Theology Today
29 Society and the Gospel

Theology Today

GENERAL EDITOR:
EDWARD YARNOLD, S.J.

No. 29

Society and
The Gospel

BY

HENRY TOWNSEND, S.J.

distributed by
CLERGY BOOK SERVICE
HALES CORNERS. WISCONSIN

ISBN 0-85342-519-1

Nihil Obstat:
Mgr. Francis Thomas, S.T.L.
19 November 1976

Imprimatur:
Mgr. D. Leonard, V.G.
Birmingham, 19 November 1976

Cum licentia superiorum ordinis

CONTENTS

ACKNOWLEDGEMENTS

The scriptural quotations in this book are taken from *The New English Bible*, copyrighted by the Oxford University Press and the Cambridge University Press, 1961 and 1970, and used by kind permission. The quotations from *The Documents of Vatican II* (ed. W.M. Abbot, S.J.) are printed by kind permission of the America Press and Geoffrey Chapman, London.

ABBREVIATIONS

DZ   H. Denzinger and A. Schönmetzer, *Enchiridion Symbolorum, Definitionum et Declarationum* (33rd ed., Barcelona etc., 1965)

Documents of Vatican II

CCMW Pastoral Constitution on the Church in the Modern World: *Gaudium et Spes*

DRF   Declaration on Religious Freedom: *Dignitatis Humanae*

Encyclicals

HV   *Humanae Vitae* (Paul VI); published by the CTS as *On the Regulation of Birth*

MM   *Mater et Magistra* (John XXIII); published by the CTS as *New Light on Social Problems*

PP   *Populorum Progressio* (Paul VI); published by the CTS as *The Great Social Problem*

PT   *Pacem in Terris* (John XXIII); published by the CTS as *Peace on Earth*

QA   *Quadragesimo Anno* (Pius XI); published by the CTS as *The Social Order*

PREFACE

The Christian revelation is good news. It brings tidings of great joy concerning the love of God and our destiny in heaven. It also brings light on human nature: 'his word our lantern is.' And, since our nature is to be social creatures, the Gospel brings us, if not a blue-print for society, at least help to understand the values that any society needs to embody.

The present book is concerned with this social Gospel. The author seeks to trace how the Church has taken the moral principles taught by Christ and elaborated them into different forms with emphases that vary according to the needs of changing conditions. Some developments, however, as one would expect, have been less true than others to the Lord's teaching.

Fr Townsend's interest in the social Gospel, which finds expression in this book, led him, when he retired from teaching at Heythrop College, to return to Rhodesia to serve the Church there. The authorities in that country, however, found his Christianity too practical for comfort, and refused him permission to stay. So he returned to London, where he met the tragic accident which brought his life to a sudden end. Perhaps those who gain help from his book will express their gratitude by praying for his soul, and for the Rhodesia to which he was so devoted.

E.J. Yarnold, S.J.

INTRODUCTION

'The joys and hopes, griefs and anxieties of people today, especially those who are poor or in any way afflicted, are also the joys and hopes, griefs and anxieties of the followers of Christ.' So spoke the Second Vatican Council at its final session in December 1965, expressing a conviction and giving a charge. Christians generally have always believed that the teaching of Christ contains a social message. Whenever their leaders have propounded principles and advocated policies for society, they have claimed to be interpreting it.

What the first Christians believed and preached is recorded in the New Testament writings. At its core is the Gospel, the good news of the liberation of men from the slavery of sin and the opening to them of a new era and prospect effected in the person of Jesus Christ who was crucified, died, was buried, and rose from the dead. For men to realize what God has made possible, they must renounce sin and put faith in Jesus Christ and none other. This basic proclamation is elaborated, with differences of elements, order and emphasis, in the four written gospels accepted and handed down by the Church as canonical or authentic accounts of one and the same Christ event.

The sayings attributed to Jesus in the gospels, even if they were not all explicitly spoken by him, represent his mind as understood by his disciples. The primitive Church was confident that, assisted by the Holy Spirit, it knew Jesus well enough to declare his mind and, following the convention of historical writing in that age, to put into his mouth words which reflected his teaching.

According to Matthew's gospel, when asked by the disciples of the Baptist, 'Are you the one who is to come, or are we to expect some other?', Jesus replied in words calling to mind the prophecies of Isaiah, 'Go and tell John what you hear and see: the blind recover their sight, the lame walk, the lepers are clean, the dead are raised to life, and the poor are hearing the good news' (Mt 11.3-5). The sign by which the promised saviour was to be recognized when he came was to be his concern for the poor and afflicted and his power to raise them up from their misery.

Yet it seems a far cry from the message of Jesus given in the gospel texts to the pronouncements of the modern Church like those of the Second Vatican Council. How is such social doctrine related to the teaching of Jesus? Does honesty compel us to say that the message of salvation recorded in the gospels has little bearing on the complex social problems of our time? Or can we claim without doing violence to Jesus' words and to our own integrity that the contemporary doctrine of the Church is rooted in the Gospel he announced?

These are not merely academic questions but questions of great practical import. The Council made an urgent appeal in the name of Christ for action to give society in process of change the direction of the Gospel. Unless we are sure that its thought represents the mind of Christ, we will hardly take its directives to heart, especially when they run counter to our inclinations and assumptions.

This book attempts to answer the question whether, or in what sense, the social teaching of the Church today is the fruit of a growing understanding of Jesus' teaching given in the gospels, or is drawn from elsewhere and read into the texts. Its method is to compare the social ideas of Jesus with what Christians have made of them, selecting a few key ideas of the New Testament writings and tracing the Church's response to them at crucial moments of its history.

For reasons of space and the author's competence, the investigation is confined to the thought of one Christian communion with which he is most familiar, the Roman Catholic Church. In the following pages the discussion up to the sixteenth century is mainly about the thought of western Christianity; after that it is concerned with the part of it which remained under the influence of the old Church. What Christians of other traditions in the East and the West have thought and done receives only oblique notice here and there. Interesting and important though a comparison between them and the tradition discussed here would be, it is beyond the scope of this book. The omission is perhaps not a grave defect. Today there is agreement between the main Christian communions on almost every important point of social doctrine.

In the text the two senses of the word 'gospel' are distinguished by upper and lower case initial letters: 'Gospel' means the basic proclamation, and 'gospel' refers to one or other of its four accepted elaborations, as indicated above. Biblical texts quoted are from the New English Bible translation.

ACKNOWLEDGEMENTS

Thanks are due to the following for permission to use copyright passages:

    Messrs Burns & Oates (J.L. Altholz: *The Liberal Catholic Movement in England*; Sidney Z. Ehler and John B. Morrall: *Church and State through the Centuries. A Collection of illustrative Documents*; Walter Shewring: *Rich and Poor in Christian Tradition*; E. Soderini: *The Pontificate of Leo XIII.*)

    Messrs Eyre & Spottiswoode (Norman A.E. St John Stevas: *The Agonizing Choice. Birth Control, Religion and the Law.*)

    Messrs Geoffrey Chapman (Walter M. Abbott: *The Documents of Vatican II.*)

    Messrs Longmans, Green & Co. (Terence Kenny: *The Political Thought of John Henry Newman*; John Henry Newman: *The Via Media of the Anglican Church.*)

    Messrs Manchester University Press (Henry Meecham: *The Epistle to Diognetus.*)

    Messrs The Tablet Publishing Co. (extracts from issues of *The Tablet* for 28 September 1969 and 16 November 1969.)

Chapter 1.
THE SOCIAL IDEAS OF THE OLD TESTAMENT

What Jesus taught, Christians have always held as intended for and of the utmost importance to every historical age. They are not on that account committed to the view that Jesus' teaching was quite independent of the particular situation in which it was first given. On the contrary, such a view is ruled out by their belief in the Bible as the inspired word of God and in Jesus as the Word made flesh. For a study of the Bible shows that from Abraham to Jesus God revealed himself to particular human beings whose culture, condition and outlook coloured the message they passed on; and Jesus, being truly human, was a Jew of his time who inherited and carried on the tradition of his people even while he revised and corrected it. Indeed, Jesus explicitly claimed to have come to complete, not to abolish, 'the Law and the Prophets' (Mt 5.17). An enquiry into the social ideas of Jesus of Nazareth must therefore begin with the Old Testament.

The span of history covered by the Old Testament is very extensive, with many different stages of social development. The Jews claimed descent from Abraham, a sheik of nomadic tribesmen who lived some 4,000 years ago with their flocks, moving from place to place in search of grazing and water much as the Bedouin still do at the present day. By the time of Jesus, about 1,800 years later, they were a settled agricultural people with a long history of religious, cultural and political growth and some degree of urban civilization. For the purpose of our enquiry it will suffice to consider a few of their moral and social ideas during that long span of time.

The Jews were one in race, culture and history with the Semites who formed part of the ancient world of the Middle East, the world of Sumer, Egypt, Phoenecia, Assyria and Babylonia. In some respects, however, they were unique. They differed from that world in their monotheistic religion and the superior moral and historical insight it gave them.

They believed that God had spoken first to Abraham, their ancestor, promising to make him the father of a great nation through which blessings for other nations would be mediated (1 Kg 18.21); then to Moses, the founder and deliverer of their nation, giving him a law for them to live by (Gen 12.2-3). God had shown himself to be the Lord of history who would bring them to a glorious destiny if they were faithful to his law. Implicit in their faith was a unique vision of history.

The universal conviction of the ancient world to which the Old Testament belongs was that from generation to generation history displays the uniform pattern of a recurring cycle of events, predetermined and irremediable. To this conviction Marcus Aurelius, Roman emperor and philosopher, gave striking expression when he said that any man of normal intelligence has already seen the past and the future by the time he is forty years old. However inconsistent with this conviction their ambitions and actions may have been, the people of the ancient world believed that human beings were tied to the wheel of history, which ran on without direction or purpose. Consequently, for them resignation to fate was the highest wisdom, and morality a matter of social conformity. Doubtless their view of history reflected men's disheartening experience of their own moral weakness and their helplessness to overcome the social ills which it engendered. To that extent it was neither fanciful nor absurd.

Alone among the nations of the epoch the Jews saw a meaning in history. To all appearances their own history was like that of other nations. It differed only in that they, being a small and weak nation, enjoyed less security and national glory than their powerful neighbours, in the rise and fall of whose empires they suffered catastrophic defeat, ruin and exile. Yet against their experience and against all apparent reason they clung obstinately to the conviction that their God was the Lord of history who had chosen them out of the nations to declare that history was meaningful and that its meaning was bound up with the destiny of their nation. Whether we realise it or not, our view of history as an evolutionary progress is derived less from the study of history than from the tradition of Europe going back through Christianity to the faith of the Jews of old. (Cf. *Faith and Freedom: A Study in Western Society*, by Barbara Ward, London 1954.)

The conviction that there was a divine plan in history and that it required their active cooperation as a people had a profound effect on the social thought and expectation of the Jews. It did not provide them with ready answers to their problems but it enabled them to see the future as something to be made, a step forward, and not as something to be passively awaited, the turn of a wheel. It left them in no doubt that the direction for their aspiration and energy was set by God's will as progressively made known to them. Consequently for them morality was not a matter of social conformity but one of attentiveness to God's voice and of openness to development.

It never entered the heads of the Jews to suppose, as Christians have sometimes been inclined to do, that morality is concerned with the private life of the individual rather than with the public concerns of society, economic and political. They shared the ancient conception of morality as essentially concerned with the community. Their religious experience of God's dealings with them confirmed it.

The faith of the Jews saved them from moral pessimism; it did not free them all at once from moral blindness and inconsistency. At many points they experienced a tension between their religious faith on the one hand and their cultural background on the other. The history of the Old Testament is largely a record of their vacillation, which shows how much they were men of their world. Even their great men betray serious moral shortcomings. A look at a few instances will help to bring the ideological background into view.

In the Bible Abraham is honoured not only as the ancestor of the Jewish people but also as the model *par excellence* of faith in God and of fidelity to God's will. He is represented as a man of high moral character and spiritual depth who became intimate with God. Yet when he took his wife, the beautiful Sarah, along with him into Egypt Abraham told her to pretend to be his sister so that he, instead of incurring the envy of Egyptian men as her husband, would win their respect and assistance as her brother. In ignorance of her true state the Pharoah took Sarah into his palace as a concubine and befriended Abraham (Gen 12.10-16). Abraham resorted to the same subterfuge when he took Sarah with him into the Negeb, and King Abimelek likewise took her into his harem. Abimelek, however, discovered the truth and was deeply aggrieved. We cannot but agree with his indignant rebuke to Abraham: 'You have done a thing that ought not to be done' (Gen 20.1-10).

Abraham feared for his life. Jacob had no such excuse. His trickery was inspired by ambition. He impersonated Esau to cheat him of the elder brother's inheritance which by Semitic custom the father's blessing conferred irrevocably on him to whom it was given (Gen 25.29-34; 27.1-45). Few of us are likely to accept St Augustine's comment: 'It is not a lie but a mystery' (*Contra Mendacium*, 9.24). We would rather say that it was a lie and a mystery, because God chose to use so faulty an instrument for his purpose.

Again, Jael, the wife of Heber the Kenite, under pretence of hospitality took in the fugitive Sisera and then killed him in his sleep. Yet the prophetess Deborah extolled Jael as 'blest above all women' for ridding Israel of a troublesome Canaanite enemy (Jdg 4.17-22; 5.25).

No doubt such passages tell of ancient tribal rivalries and wars. But at the same time they reveal something of the mentality of that age. Men of alien nations were regarded as inferiors and every trick to doublecross them if they were enemies was not only applauded but even approved as right and a deed of religious value. The consciousness of the Jews that they had been chosen by God to be his special agents in history evidently did little to widen their horizon. Rather, it constituted a temptation for them to identify their national ambitions with God's will and to condemn those who thwarted them as enemies of God himself. The attitude of the Jews at that date to deceit and cunning as a means of furthering the aims of the family, tribe and nation appears to have been much the same as that of the Homeric warriors who respected the wily Odysseus for his ability to outwit and cheat not only the Trojans but also his fellow Greeks. He was honoured as an exceptionally shrewd and resourceful man.

We are amused by Odysseus but shocked by Jacob. For Jacob is commemorated as a man chosen by God to carry his plan of salvation forward, whereas Odysseus is only a legendary figure and a hero in quite another sense. Our shock is largely of our own making. We bring to the Old Testament the moral insights of a later and more developed date, especially those imparted by Jesus Christ in the New Testament. We assume that when God speaks to men the normal processes of human learning and understanding are somehow bypassed, so that the minds of those with whom he communicates are in a flash enlightened so fully that everything is at once made clear: not only the immediate message but also what is related to it, the whole moral law. All the evidence of the Bible is against such an assumption; and our experience of our own moral development gives it no support.

Even more disconcerting is the attitude of the Old Testament patriarchs to brutality. Joshua's behaviour at the fall of Jericho is perhaps the most notorious case. In the Bible Joshua is presented as a great and good man 'filled with the spirit of wisdom, for Moses had laid his hands on him' (Deut 34.9). Yet it was he who ordered the total destruction of the city and all its inhabitants because Jericho had held out against the Israelites, blocking their passage into the land or promise. 'Shout,' he ordered. 'The Lord has given you the city. The city shall be under solemn ban: everything in it belongs to the Lord' (Josh 6.17,21). What to us appears as vindictive brutality was evidently regarded and undertaken by Joshua as an act of religion.

The Semites of that epoch looked upon resistance by the enemy in time of war as opposition not only to their nation but also to its gods, under whose protection and for whose glory battle was joined. For the Jews at that date there was also another motive for 'devoting to destruction' the Canaanite cities which were strong enough to hold out against them. As they settled down among the Canaanites they ran the risk of religious and moral contamination, and when they encountered determined resistance they felt that their mono-theism and its high moral code were at stake.

Joshua, we may conclude, was a good man in that he sought to do God's will, but was mistaken in what he took God's will to be. For a man of that society his judgment, though erroneous, was neither capricious nor merely savage. The same may be said of Samuel's condemnation of Saul for sparing the life of Agag, king of the Amelekites, whose city the prophet had put under ban (1 Sam 15.1-33).

It is significant that in the book of Judges, covering the first two centuries of Jewish occupation of Canaan, no further mention is made of 'the ban', the sacrificial destruction of whole cities and their inhabitants. Instead of extermination we read of exaction of forced labour as the penalty imposed on the vanquished.

Forced labour meant slavery. To avoid the fate of Jericho, the men of Gibeon surrendered to Joshua. He spared their lives, but made them hewers of wood and drawers of water for the Jews (Josh 9.3-27). From the books of Exodus, Leviticus and Deuteronomy it is clear that slavery became a regular feature of Jewish society. As long as the Jews were nomads they had no interest in it; but once they acquired land and settled down as farmers they took to it.

Slavery was a universal institution of the ancient world. It appears to have gone unquestioned as the only effective means of exacting reparation in time of war and of making good bad debts in time of peace. Only by controlling the labour, and therefore the persons, of those who were held to have inflicted them could losses be recovered. So conceived enslavement was not divorced from considerations of justice. But because it was profitable, it became a permanent form of exploitation.

Jewish law did not forbid slavery but sought to control its practice and mitigate its harshness. It followed closely one of the most enlightened legal codes of the ancient world, the code of Hammurabi, king of Babylon in the time of Abraham (Cf. *Documents of Old Testament Times*, ed. D. Winton Thomas, London 1958, pp. 27-37). Slaves were not an absolute possession but retained some rights. In some of its prescriptions Jewish law was more liberal than Hammurabi's code. For example, if a slave suffered grievous bodily harm at the hands of his master, Jewish law granted him his freedom, whereas Hammurabi's code compensated him by a sum of money (Exod 21.26-7). Special consideration was given to slaves who were Jews. Though they, like foreign slaves, could be bought and sold and inherited, the term of their servitude was limited to six years, and masters were bound to treat them as members of the household. In the seventh year, the 'sabbatical' year, masters had to emancipate them and moreover endow them against destitution. The Jews were constantly reminded by their sacred writings that they had once been slaves and had been liberated from the Egyptians by the intervention of God. This sacred memory of God's compassion inculcated an attitude of humanity which benefited foreign slaves as well (Ex 21.2; Lev 25.39-46; Deut 15.12-18).

If in general the Jews had a more acute sense of justice than other nations, it was due to their religious faith and to a few remarkable men. The prophets were active especially during periods of great material prosperity, which turned the heads of the Jews, and periods of national catastrophe, which threw them into despair. They spoke out like the voice of conscience denouncing the sins of society, especially religious hypocrisy and economic exploitation. The remedy they advocated was a return to the love of God and the keeping of his law. For them righteousness (including justice in the modern sense) was not only a duty imposed by religion but identical with true religion. In both the Old and the New Testaments 'righteousness' goes deeper than 'justice'; it is not satisfied by conformity of social behaviour to legally prescribed norms and accepted principles of equity, but requires also an inner quality of loyalty, service and compassion of person to person, modelled on the faithfulness of God to his people which was manifested in history especially by his saving acts in its times of adversity. Jeremiah made the point unmistakably clear when he represented God as commending the just rule of King Josiah in the words: 'He dispensed justice to the lowly and poor; did not this show he knew me? says the Lord' (Jer 22.16).

Amos made the same point, only more bluntly. Challenging the capitalist practices of Samaria during a period of unprecedented affluence, he declared that the Lord would punish the men 'because they sell the innocent for silver and the destitute for a pair of shoes' (Amos 2.6) and also the women, 'cows of Bashan who live on the hills of Samaria' (the select suburbs) and 'oppress the poor and crush the destitute' (Amos 4.1). About the same time Micah spoke out against encroachment by the rich on the property of the poor in the southern kingdom of Judah. He denounced in particular the assumption that power confers right: 'Shame on those who lie in bed planning . . . wicked deeds and rise at daybreak to do them, knowing that they have the power. They covet land and take it by force; if they want a house they seize it; they rob a man of his home and steal every man's inheritance' (Micah 2.1-2).

What the prophets denounced was not that the northern kingdom had grown rich on agriculture nor that the southern kingdom had prospered on trade, but that neither recognised that God was concerned with these activities. They declared that God is the Lord of economics and politics no less than of religion. Their denunciations were prompted not by mere conservatism but by a refusal to condone a social order which made a mockery of godliness and religion by neglecting the claims of humanity.

As long as the Jewish nation lived, righteousness and sin were social conceptions, and the preaching of the prophets made a point of condemning social injustice as a crime which made nonsense of the worship of the Lord. But once the life of the nation was destroyed by the disaster of exile and subjection to the Babylonians, the stress of prophetic preaching changed. It was then laid on personal responsibility before God. When the individual came to realise that he was personally dear to God and could work out his salvation by his own fidelity to God's law in circumstances which deprived him of the stimulus and support of his tribe and nation, religion and morality stood to gain. But then there threatened the danger that religion and morality might be divorced from social concern and become individualistic.

To that danger the Jews did not completely succumb. Instead, their religious outlook took on a formalism which blunted their social sense. To keep the Jews true to the Lord and his covenant in the pagan environment of Babylon, the exilic prophets laid great stress on the ritual prescriptions of the Mosaic law. Ezekiel especially fired Jewish hopes by describing in the form of a vision a new Jerusalem and a new temple with elaborate ceremonial which they were to build on their return from exile. This emphasis so influenced Jewish thinking that in later years righteousness came to be increasingly equated with fidelity to external observance. The letter came to matter more than the spirit of the law, and exact performance of its prescriptions more than human need. It would, however, be unfair to blame Ezekiel for this distortion. He aspired to restore the nation, a social aim, to which liturgical and legal observance was a necessary means. So far was he from losing sight of social justice that he made provision in his planning for a fair distribution of land among the people when they should return to their country (Ezek 47.13,21-3; 48.1-7,23-9). In the eyes of Ezekiel, as of all the prophets, religious renewal and social reconstruction were identical aims. The Jews did not distinguish between the 'spiritual' and the 'secular'. For them human beings and their societies were unities of both, and both had to be brought into the service of God.

The Jews never lost hope in the future. Though their hope underwent changes with the vicissitudes of their history, it remained basically the same hope in the Lord's promise. As they passed from tribal organisation to nationhood, it took on a wider perspective. When their national expectations were frustrated by adversity and defeat, it became more individual. And when their political autonomy and liberty were swept away by exile, it became more transcendent and apocalyptic, less concerned with present events and more concerned with their ultimate future.

The corollary of a hope which is individual, personal, is that it is universal: a hope for everybody without distinction of origin and condition. This conclusion was not generally accepted. The prophets, especially the exilic prophets Deutero-Isaiah and Ezekiel, expected and preached that one day all nations would come to see that Israel's God is the only God, and be included in the hope for Israel. In the psalms too this is a recurring theme. But the dominant view was that the Gentiles were simply godless, and with it went the hope that when the Messianic kingdom arrived God would destroy Israel's oppressors utterly. Even after the exile the Jewish people as a whole continued to be more concerned with the promise that as Abraham's children they would become a great nation than with the promise that as God's agents in history they would bring a blessing to all nations. Consequently, the exclusiveness of their hope in the future narrowed their conception of social justice in the present to their own nation.

Chapter 2.
THE SOCIAL MESSAGE OF JESUS

Jesus, like the Baptist, began his preaching with the dramatic announcement 'Repent; for the kingdom of heaven is upon you' (Mt 4.17). To understand what these words meant to the Jews of the time and why they caused excitement we have to recall what the general expectation was.

From the eighth century B.C. the Jewish people had suffered one political disaster after another. The kingdom united under David broke up into two, each part going it alone and in turn falling foul of its powerful neighbours. Israel in the north, after flourishing for a time, was crushed by Assyria and its people were taken into captivity, never to return. Judah in the south lasted longer but in the end suffered a like fate at the hands of the Babylonians. The rise of Persia terminated the captivity of the Judaeans, and returning to their homeland they rebuilt it, only to be overrun by Alexander and his Greeks. A successful revolt led by the Maccabees freed Judah for a while, but internal quarrels and civil disorder led to the intervention of Rome, which took over control of the country.

In these disasters the Jewish prophets saw the judgment of God on his perverse people, who for the destiny to which he had called them had substituted one of their own choosing. Each in his own way, the prophets contrasted the infidelity of the Jews to the Lord with the Lord's unswerving fidelity to his promise. But while they denounced the prevailing sins of ir-religion, worldly ambition and social injustice, they pointed forward to a good time coming when the Lord would reign over the whole earth. After the fall of Jerusalem the dominant Jewish hope was that God would establish his own sovereignty by restoring the former Davidic kingdom, and the expectation grew that he would raise up a Messiah, an anointed king of the Jews, to be his agent.

Prophecy became more and more explicit. The Messiah would be a king sprung from David's royal line. The spirit of the Lord would rest upon him filling him with wisdom and

23

understanding. Swayed by no human partiality he would rule over the people with justice and defend the humble of the land with equity. And, uniting Israel and Judah again, he would lead his people to triumph over the nations to the West, the East, the South and the North (Is 11.1-16).

Jesus certainly regarded the founding of a kingdom as the special work for which he had been sent by his Father. To the people of Capernaum, who pressed him to stay with them, he replied: 'I must give the good news of the kingdom of God to the other towns also, for that is what I was sent to do' (Lk 4.43). The good news, the Gospel, was that the kingdom of heaven had arrived.

Yet Jesus never applied the title of Messiah to himself. He did not refuse it but made little of it and was on his guard when other people applied it to him. He preferred to call himself by a title without overtones, 'the Son of Man' (e.g. Mk 8.27-31; Jn 1.49-51). One reason for his caution may have been that in the minds of the Jews the wish was father to the thought that the promised Messiah would be a political saviour who would be quite literally another David, a national leader who would reunite them, drive out the new Philistines, the Romans, and establish a strong Jewish kingdom to stand forever, wielding dominion over the whole world. This was the expectation of the Zealots, the nationalist activist party, who had a numerous following. Among the immediate followers of Jesus was at least one Zealot, Simon, named with that title in the gospels (Lk 6.15; Acts 1.13). According to a well known scholar of today there may have been others (Cf. O. Cullmann, *The State in the New Testament*, London 1963, Ch. 1). Perhaps Judas Iscariot, since 'Iscariot' may have been an Aramaic form of the Latin *sicarius* (terrorist). Perhaps James and John, 'sons of thunder'. Perhaps even Peter; for he always had a sword handy. However that may be, the danger of being taken for the kind of Messiah the Zealots expected was too great for Jesus to ignore. Such a misunderstanding would have been fatal to his mission. It would have completely misrepresented the purpose of his preaching: salvation through a death and resurrection.

24

None the less, Jesus did claim kingship. When at the close of his life he stood before the Roman governor on the charge of sedition, he admitted to being a king; but he took pains to explain that his kingship was not of this world. Were it of this world, he said, his followers would be under arms and fighting to rescue him (Jn 19.33-8). If we are to understand Jesus' social teaching we must first understand what exactly he meant.

It is sometimes said that the kingdom of heaven is the reign of God in the souls of men. Jesus certainly demanded of his followers a total surrender involving a change of heart. This is clear from the whole tenor of his teaching and is summed up in several striking texts in the gospels, such as the following. 'None of you can be a disciple of mine without taking leave of all his possessions' (Lk 14.33). 'No servant can be a slave of two masters: for either he will hate the first and love the second, or he will be devoted to the first and think nothing of the second. You cannot serve God and money' (Mt 6.24). Most striking of all: 'If anyone wishes to be a follower of mine, he must leave self behind; he must take up his cross and come with me. Whoever cares for his own safety is lost; but if a man will let himself be lost for my sake, he will find his true self. What will a man gain by winning the whole world, at the cost of his true self?' (Mt 16.24-5).

A number of sayings suggest that the kingdom of God is not yet present but a future event. So Jesus bids his followers pray: 'Thy kingdom come.' Others seem to envisage a kingdom to be realised only at the end of human history. This is the suggestion, for example, of the parable of the wise and the foolish virgins, the parable of the talents, and the account of the great assize of mankind at the end of time when the Son of Man will say to the good: 'Come, enter and possess the kingdom that has been ready for you since the world was made' (Mt 25.1-46).

From texts like these some Christians have drawn the conclusion that Jesus was not concerned with the present world but only with a world which follows death, and that his whole aim was to raise men's thoughts above the affairs of this life and fix them on a better life to come. An extreme variant of this interpretation is that Jesus was positively opposed to all that concerns the state and its jurisdiction and that he would not have his followers participate in civil government or submit to its laws.

In the latter part of his career Jesus does seem to have turned his thoughts more and more from the things of this life to 'the last things': some future state of things which would follow his 'parousia' or coming in triumph at the end of time, an event which his disciples believed, or hoped, would occur soon. But it does not follow from his preoccupation with 'the last things' that Jesus was indifferent to the affairs of this life or opposed to social concern. His aim must be construed from his teaching as a whole. Other parables and sayings about the kingdom give a different impression.

Jesus certainly meant that the kingdom of heaven has its beginning on earth. He opened his public career with the announcement that the kingdom is 'at hand', present; and he instructed his disciples to make the same proclamation (Mt 10.7-8). After the death of John the Baptist Jesus, speaking in his praise, concluded: 'Yet the least in the kingdom of heaven is greater than he. Ever since the coming of John the Baptist the kingdom of heaven has been subjected to violence and violent men are seizing it' (Mt 11.11-13). More explicit still was his answer to the question when the kingdom would come: 'You cannot tell by observation when the kingdom of God comes. There will be no saying "Look, here it is!" or "there it is"; for in fact the kingdom of God is among you' (Lk 17.20-27).

Significantly, the operation of the kingdom is described in terms of growth, from small beginnings and in dependence upon human factors. It is to develop like grain planted in a field, or like a tiny mustard seed, or like a vine (Mk 4.26-31; 12.1). Its development can be impeded by the kind of soil in which it has to grow (Mk 4.3-8), or by obstacles put in its way by opponents (Mt 13.25), or by the infidelity of the Master's servants who turn it to their own temporal advantage (Mk 12.1-9). In other words, the kingdom is an ideal to be realised by a process of growth: like some new kind of life springing up within the old, not destroying but transforming it and working from within outwards.

The kingdom of God, though a kingdom of the spirit, is in some sense a visible kingdom. What that sense is may be gathered from the practice of Jesus and his followers. In the gospels the kingdom begins to take shape as a community of disciples, especially the Twelve, gathered round Jesus, and is seen to have a social character and aim. It is not a community withdrawn from the everyday world and indifferent to its affairs, but a community active in the world and devoted to its transformation. It acts on the world like yeast on flour (Lk 13.20-21). So Jesus said and did.

In his own village of Nazareth Jesus applied to himself the messianic text of Isaiah, 'The spirit of the Lord is upon me because he has anointed me. He has sent me to announce the good news to the poor, to proclaim release for prisoners and recovery of sight for the blind; to let the broken victims go free, to proclaim the year of the Lord's favour' (Lk 4.18-19). Much of Jesus' popularity with the crowds was due to the fact that as he went about preaching he gave sympathetic attention to their troubles and needs, healing their ills of mind and body and raising their hopes. Behind modern humanitarianism lies the compassion of Christ which through the centuries his followers, for all their shortcomings, have imitated successfully enough to produce a new sensibility in mankind.

Nothing in the gospels is more evident than that Jesus recognised the need of reform, individual and social. He was not a reformer of the sort who aims directly at improving the laws and institutions by which society is governed and administered; but the change of mind and heart to which he called men would, if undertaken, inevitably though indirectly bring about a transformation of the social order. He had none of the impatience of the social reformer in the modern sense. Only on rare occasions did he show that indignation at social evils which wants to turn society upside down, and then what stirred his anger was hypocrisy and profiteering in religion. It was not the slave-owners nor the tax-gatherers nor the dishonest stewards whom he lashed with his tongue and whipped out with cords, but the Pharisees for their self-righteousness and the money-changers for exploiting piety within the temple precincts. Such abuses make a mockery of religion and turn men away from God.

Accordingly, the Christian reformer is not a man of violence working for a sudden upheaval of society but a man of patience and hope working for the interpenetration of men and society by a new spirit. That is not to say that drastic action is never to be taken. Sometimes the tree must be cut down because it merely encumbers the ground and is incapable of bearing fruit. But the decision to take drastic action should not be hasty (Lk 13.6-9). This use of the parable of the unfruitful fig-tree does not miss its point (that God in his justice has already passed sentence on Israel for infidelity but in his mercy through Christ grants Israel a last opportunity for repentance) but applies it as a principle for human conduct (since God's dealing with men is the model for men's dealing with one another).

Rightly recognising that Jesus was deeply concerned with the affairs of this life, some Christians have gone so far as to think that his whole ideal was to establish a paradise on earth through social welfare, seeing in him a social reformer rather than a religious saviour. Such an interpretation is as untenable as the opposed view that Jesus had no interest in the affairs of this life at all. It reflects the preoccupation of those who hold it rather than the full significance of Jesus himself. But it has this much merit that in emphasizing his social concern it helps to redress the imbalance of a purely 'eschatological' interpretation.

Each of these views reflects a genuine aspect of Jesus' teaching and misrepresents it only in claiming to take in the whole of it. Jesus was indeed deeply concerned with the affairs of this life; but for him they are affairs which have a bearing on human welfare not only on earth but also, and especially, in heaven. So understood, his teaching is seen to have both an individual or 'spiritual' message and a social message which are not in conflict but complementary. In this it is entirely realistic: it meets the needs of human nature.

Every person, being both an individual and a member of society, leads his own private life and at the same time shares in the corporate life of the community. He can no more forgo the one than the other; but he can neglect one for the other, becoming either a self-centred individualist or an impersonal collectivist. A sound social doctrine must accommodate both these tendencies of human nature, not by cutting them back but by unifying them. This Jesus' teaching makes possible by providing a common aim for both, so that by reaching out in the same direction they can be made to work harmoniously together. It seeks to bring about a change in men, a conversion of heart and mind (the basic meaning of 'repentance') which will draw them into the right relation with God and with one another, thereby introducing them into a new kind of life beginning on earth and reaching full maturity in heaven. That life is to be a life of love, initiated and sustained by God: love for God issuing in, and measured by, love of man for man. Thus the kingdom which Jesus announced is an interior kingdom, but an interior kingdom which is to overflow into men's relations with one another.

Jesus was at pains to stress that his commandment of love has no limits to its scope or to its measure. His followers are to recognize that God is the Father not only of themselves but also of others, and that they are to love as their brothers even their enemies and persecutors. 'You have learned that they (their forefathers) were told, "love your neighbour, hate your enemy". But what I tell you is this: Love your enemies and pray for your persecutors; only so can you be children of your heavenly Father, who makes his sun shine on good and bad alike, and sends the rain on the honest and the dishonest' (Mt 5.43-8). At the great assize at the end of time all will be judged by the same test of mutual love and service. To each the king will say, 'I tell you this: anything you did for one of my brothers here, however humble, you did for me' (Mt 25.31-41).

In the New Testament the word 'brothers' refers as a rule to the disciples of Jesus and is almost a technical term for them. But in these sayings Jesus gives it a universal extension. He identifies himself, the king, not only with his followers but also with all men and especially the unfortunate. On another occasion, in answer to the question 'Who is my neighbour?' he underlined his meaning in a striking parable (Lk 10.25-37).

The lesson of the story of the Good Samaritan is unmistakably clear: the essence of true religion lies not in exactness of religious observance (the priest and the Levite) but in generosity of practical service without limits (the Samaritan). Jesus deliberately introduced a Samaritan as hero to emphasize the lengths to which love must go in regard both to the persons it embraces and to the services it renders. For the Jews despised and avoided the Samaritans as a depraved and inferior people, displaying in this much of the mentality of *apartheid*.

The disciples of Jesus learned his meaning above all from his own manner of life and death. It was to this that the earliest Christian exhortations appealed: 'It is by this that we know what love is: that Christ laid down his life for us. And we in our turn are bound to lay down our lives for our brothers. But if a man has enough to live on, and yet when he sees his brother in need shuts up his heart against him, how can it be said that love for God dwells in him?' (1 Jn 3.16-17)

Was Jesus' teaching new? In his farewell discourse to his disciples as recounted by John Jesus said: 'I give you a new commandment: love one another; as I have loved you, so you are to love one another. If there is this love among you, then all will know that you are my disciples' (Jn 13.34-5). But love was enjoined by the Law of the Old Testament, quite explicitly in two places. 'Hear, O Israel, the Lord is our God, one Lord, and you must love the Lord your God with all your heart and soul and strength.' 'You shall not nurse hatred against your brother . . ., you shall love your neighbour as a man like yourself' (Deut 6.4-5; Lev 19.18). This Jesus acknowledged, quoting these two texts in reply to the lawyer's question as to which of the commandments of the Law mattered most, and concluding with the remark, 'Everything in the Law and the prophets hangs on these two commandments' (Mt 22.36-40). On another occasion he made the same point thus: 'Always treat others as you would like them to treat you: that is the Law and the prophets' (Mt 7.12).

Jesus' teaching here is new only in that it propounds the two commandments as the very principle of the Torah, the Law and the prophets, giving it a universal extension and setting it a standard of perfection by his own example. In other words, his teaching aims not only at leading men's minds back to a recognition of the principle of God's law but also at leading them forward to a deeper understanding of the principle itself. Henceforth, to love our neighbour means to love even those who harm and oppress us; to forgive those who offend and injure us not only sometimes but at all times; to turn the other cheek to those who attack us; to be open-handed, giving one of our coats to him who has none; to take the lowest place at a gathering in deference to other people; so to esteem other people as to be unwilling to condemn them; and to be ready even to lay down our lives for their sakes.

Indubitably, Jesus' ethical doctrine is primarily concerned with the personal attitude and conduct of one man to another; but it is not for that reason individualistic, without relevance to the affairs and problems of economics, politics and the state. Jesus wanted men to live righteously in common; but only in so far as social affairs involved questions of moral principle did he deal with them, and then only as they confronted him.

His references to wealth and poverty are a case in point. He stressed directly the spiritual dangers of large possessions rather than the social evils of maldistribution of property, but in such a way as to turn the accepted scale of values upside down. In the Sermon on the Mount it is the poor, not the rich, who are congratulated (Mt 5.3). To the rich he gave a solemn warning, reiterated with dramatic emphasis in the parable of Dives and Lazarus (Lk 16.19-31). There is no suggestion that Dives, the rich man, had acquired his wealth dishonestly or was anything but a respectable citizen in the eyes of the world. Yet he is condemned, and with him all the well-to-do who are blind to the plight of the poor at their gates. The lesson is the same as the Old Testament prophets taught. One of the masses himself, Jesus knew from experience what it is to be poor in a world which honours and is run by the rich. He did not preach class-war but again and again insisted on a radical change in men and society. It is not enough for the rich to give generously. All must undergo a change in spirit and scale of values. Thus indirectly Jesus demanded radical change in the distribution of property and the whole social order.

Though one of them himself, Jesus was not blind to the faults of the working-class. He adverted to them in the parable of the vineyard, for example (Mt 20.1-16). Even if the point of the parable is God's free disposal of his grace, it is made by commending the employer's generosity and condemning the envy and greed of employees who are paid an agreed and just wage.

It is less easy to discover Jesus' mind on political questions. The circumstances of the time demanded reticence if Jesus was to avoid exciting the expectations of the Zealots and the suspicions of the Romans. There are, however, hints enough in the gospels if we read between the lines.

Jesus refused to take sides for or against the nationalist cause. The tears he shed over the fate which he foresaw for Jerusalem leave no room for doubt about his deep feeling for his own people, but he repudiated the Zealots' belief in the primacy of politics and advised people to set their minds on 'God's kingdom and his justice before everything else, and all the rest will come to you as well.' He acknowledged that men have duties to the state as well as to God, but also cautioned the state in the person of the Roman governor that its authority comes from God and that those whose office it is to exercise power over others are responsible to God for its use (Mk 12.13-17; Jn 19.10-11). He openly described Herod, ruler of Galilee, as 'that fox', which looks like forthright political criticism (Lk 13.32). He spoke out in irony about the custom of rulers to give themselves the high sounding title of 'benefactor of the people' though they ruled by force (Lk 22.25-6). From such utterances we may gather something of Jesus' mind. His words do not suggest that he favoured silence and acquiescence at all times. But it is to the principles and attitudes which he inculcated rather than to his explicit statements that we must look for political guidance.

One incident recorded in the gospels is of special importance. Jesus was asked if it was right for Jews to pay the poll-tax imposed by the Romans. This tax was extremely unpopular both because it was a constant reminder to the Jews of their subject status and because the silver coinage in which it was paid bore the name and image of Caesar. The question was well calculated to embarrass Jesus whichever way he answered it. If he advised payment he would discredit himself in the eyes of all who favoured the Zealots, by whom he would be branded as a traitor to the nationalist cause; and if he pronounced against it he would offend those who favoured tolerating the *status quo* and collaborating with the Romans, to whom they would delate him. Jesus escaped through the horns of the dilemma by his celebrated reply: 'Pay Caesar what is due to Caesar, and pay God what is due to God' (Mt 22.15-22; Mk 12.13-17; Lk 20.21-6).

These words are more widely remembered than understood. They are commonly misconstrued, as though Jesus were distributing human obligations between duties to Caesar and duties to God, thereby dividing human life into two separate spheres. So understood, strange views may find support in the gospels. It may even be argued that in public life morality is identical with legality, or that normal rules of morality do not apply to public actions. That is precisely what Jesus did not say. Had he done so, he would have fallen into the trap set for him by siding with the collaborationists, giving colour to their belief that Caesar was God's counterpart. What he did say was that men must give the state what it has a right to demand, the taxes and cooperation which every state needs to carry out its proper functions, and give to God what is his, the whole of their life and loyalty. In Jesus' reply there is thus a disguised challenge: if ever the state oversteps the limits of its authority and hinders the proclamation and living out of the Gospel, then resist it! Hence, the followers of Christ have the right and duty to judge the state by the Gospel, a duty of political criticism. They may never entrust their conscience to the officers of the state, whether in time of peace or in time of war.

Jesus did not furnish an exact definition of what is Caesar's and what is God's. Inevitably, borderline disputes will occur. They are to be settled in the light of the Gospel as a whole and in the spirit it engenders. But Jesus was clearly opposed to the tendency of the state to make totalitarian claims on its subjects, demanding their total life and loyalty which belong to God alone. For that reason too, we may infer, Jesus was opposed to nationalism of the extreme form which the Zealots promoted. Identifying it with 'the Law and the prophets' they gave it divine pretensions.

Jesus respected human liberty and sought to win men by persuasion. He firmly rejected the tempter's suggestion that he should initiate the kingdom of God on earth by means of a sensational impact on men's minds: casting himself down from the parapet of the temple in sight of the crowds below, to be borne gently to the ground by angels (Mt 4.5-7). Instead, he identified himself with the masses of ordinary people and began his public career by taking his place in the queue to be baptized at the hands of John (Mt 3.13). To convince his hearers that he came from God and spoke with God's authority, he invited them to study the scriptures and reflect on his deeds (Jn 5.39;10.38). He spoke with such authority that the people were deeply impressed, but he did not try to compel their consent and compliance (Mt 7.28-9). Indeed, he expressly warned his followers against the temptation of those in authority to resort to compulsion: 'You know that in the world rulers lord it over their subjects, and that their great men make them feel the weight of their authority; but it shall not be so with you. Among you, whoever wants to be great must be the willing slave of all—like the Son of Man; he did not come to be served, but to serve, and to give up his life as a ransom for many' (Mt 20.25-8; Mk 10.42-5).

The standard of respect for human freedom set by Jesus his followers have more often than not been slow to make their own. Too often they have done no better than accept the

34

standards of the day, and sometimes they have not scrupled to use intimidation and force to further evangelical aims. The fault of Christians has not been that they were worse than their contemporaries, but that they were not conspicuously better.

Freedom, not constraint, is the atmosphere of the kingdom of God because fraternity, not fear, is its bond. Yet nowhere in the gospels is it recorded that Jesus spoke out against slavery which, more than any other practice of the ancient world, denied the brotherhood and essential equality of men and withheld liberty from very many. This silence has puzzled many, and even encouraged some opponents of social reconstruction in their illiberal opinions.

Slavery continued among the Jews in New Testament times, though on a smaller scale and with more humanity than elsewhere (Cf. R. de Vaux, *Ancient Israel*, London, ed. 2, 1965, passim). In the gospels Jesus is seen to be aware of the practice around him and to advert to it openly, not in condemnation of it but in illustration of his teaching; for the royal and baronial households in which slavery continued offered in some ways an analogy with the kingdom of God. For example, in the parables of the householder who planted a vineyard and of the great wedding feast the 'servants' and 'stewards' of our translations were domestic slaves (Mt 21.33-43; 22.1-14). In the first parable they stand for the Jews, as the priests and Pharisees were quick to recognise; in the second they represent the prophets in the Old Testament and the apostles in the New who were sent by God as his messengers to invite first the Jews, then the Gentiles, into his kingdom.

The relation between his disciples and himself Jesus repeatedly described as that of servants or slaves to their lord or master. But he also stressed the inadequacy of the figure by taking upon himself the role of a slave in washing the feet of the Twelve (Jn 13.2-17) and, at the close of his life, by declaring them emancipated: 'I call you servants [slaves] no longer; a servant [slave] does not know what his master is about. I have called you friends, because I have disclosed to you everything that I have heard from my Father' (Jn 15.15). Thus the human division between bondmen and freemen, slaves and masters, becomes meaningless in the community of Christ. Because its citizens are sons of the same Father, and therefore brothers, the kingdom of God is a classless society in which all are equal and free. Distinction lies not in birth or wealth or natural talent but in service and self-sacrifice. To the sons of Zebedee, James and John, for whom their mother asked positions of power and privilege in the kingdom of God, Jesus offered only the cup of endurance (Mt 20.20-23).

As long as a man's social possibilities to be realised in this life are thought to constitute his entire claim to consideration, a system of some sort of *apartheid* (slavery, subordination of classes, segregation of races, etc.) is a logical if cruel consequence. But once it is admitted that men possess a worth and dignity which is theirs not only on the ground of their common nature but also and chiefly in virtue of the Father's love and design for them all, then they have a moral claim to equal consideration and opportunity. Thus in the doctrine of the Fatherhood of God and the brotherhood of men lies the whole basis and force of the socially regenerative work of Jesus, one result of which has been that slavery came to be seen as monstrous and finally disappeared.

The Jews spoke of the Fatherhood of God and the Stoics proclaimed the brotherhood of men before the time of Jesus. What he taught was not altogether unprecedented. But in revealing the nature of the Father in his own person and the brotherhood of men in his own example, and linking the two doctrines inextricably together, Jesus gave both an immeasurably deeper meaning, individual and social. The fact that all men are children in the one family of God cannot but throw light on the relations which ought to exist between one man and another and between individual men and society.

Chapter 3.
THE FIRST CENTURIES

For appreciation of the social message of the Gospel the early centuries of Christianity are obviously of great importance. The first churches were then taking shape, and whatever we can learn about them is valuable evidence of how the disciples of Jesus Christ, many of whom had heard and known him in the flesh, understood his teaching to apply to the business of everyday life. The records they left are scanty, but informative enough to give us a fair outline picture with some reliable details.

It is clear that from the outset Christianity was not only a doctrine but also a way of life and above all a society of believers which took concrete form in a number of local communities in close association with one another. The first of these in time and place was the church at Jerusalem about which we read in the early chapters of the Acts of the Apostles and in the pastoral Letters. Like the city it was cosmopolitan, but unlike the city it cut across natural and conventional lines of social cleavage (Acts 2.9-11; Col 3.11). There, as elsewhere in later years, rich and poor, masters and slaves, lawyers and fishermen, members of the governing class and peasants, all mixed together on a footing of equality not only for worship but also 'to share the common life' (Acts 2.42). What Paul said of the church at Corinth was no doubt true also of the church at Jerusalem: it included few people of high education, few of the powerful and well born, many who were by this world's standards 'low and contemptible, mere nothings' (1 Cor 1.26-8). The only bond which tied such heterogeneous elements into one community was a common faith and a common desire to live as brothers witnessing to the world as Jesus Christ had commanded.

Jesus' call to give up home and possessions, reputation and prospects in this life for his sake, which was treasured in the collection of his sayings out of which the gospels grew, corresponded to the actual experience of his disciples, especially

at Jerusalem. To be a follower of Jesus of Nazareth was not so much to cut oneself off from the life of the city as to incur official suspicion and risk of arrest for subversion. At first the disciples continued to take part in the temple services and to gather in its cloisters for discussion. But nobody who was not one of them ventured to join in (Acts 5.13). Even if Luke's description is idealized, there is no reason to doubt that a remarkable spirit of unity and brotherhood, assisted by isolation, flourished in the community and expressed itself in voluntary communism: 'All those whose faith had drawn them together held everything in common; they would sell their property and possessions and make a general distribution as the need of each required' (Acts 2.44; 4.32-5).

Barnabas is singled out for mention as a rich man who sold his estate and handed over the proceeds to the apostles for the benefit of the Christian community. Ananias and his wife on the other hand incurred severe condemnation, not for holding something back but for pretending to have given all so as to win a reputation for great generosity (Acts 4.36-7; 5.1-12). Peter did not exaggerate the gravity of Ananias' trickery. It was nothing less than hypocrisy, and hypocrisy was fatal to brotherhood and the whole Christian way of life.

The communism of the primitive church in Jerusalem had as its motive not an economic theory but a religious ideal. It was prompted by Jesus' example and recommendation to sell one's property and give the money to the poor in order to be perfect in the kingdom of God (Mk 10.21,25; Lk 12.33; 6.20,24). Such was the first Christians' devotion to Jesus and their spirit of brotherhood that they took his words literally. There is something splendid about their communism which would continue to haunt the minds of generous Christians down the centuries. However, experience proved that it was unworkable as a way of life for everyone.

After a time the Jerusalem community found itself without any economic resources. For not only had it exhausted the endowment of its few rich members, but, counting on the imminent return of Jesus Christ in glory to bring human history on earth to a close, it had neglected economic enter-

prise and planning for the future. This expectation was a form of wishful thinking which Paul found it necessary to correct in the Thessalonians. He admonished them not to be carried away by excitement at the prospect of the life to come but 'to work quietly for their living' because the date of the Lord's coming was uncertain (2 Thess 2.1-3; 3.12).

In its penury the Jerusalem community turned for assistance to the daughter churches abroad where Christians were less hampered and better off. As apostle to the Gentiles, Paul made it his business to collect funds 'for the relief of the poor among God's people at Jerusalem', appealing to the churches of Galatia, Macedonia, Achaia and Rome for regular contributions (Gal 2.10; 1 Cor 16.1; 2 Cor 9.1; Rom 15.26). A few years later severe persecution, in which the deacon Stephen fell a victim to mob violence (Acts 7.57-8.3), scattered the church of Jerusalem, and the practice of common ownership ended. In its place was substituted a system of contributing alms regularly to a common fund administered by the local 'president', or bishop, as we learn from a writing addressed to the emperor Trajan by Justin, who had made a tour of the churches up and down the Mediterranean world (1 *Apol.*, 65; 67.5-6).

What came to be the standard Christian attitude to property is given by Clement Alexandria (A.D. 150-210), head of one of the earliest theological schools: 'Sell your belongings! What does that mean? It is not, as some too readily interpret it, a command to get rid of what belongs to you and abandon your property; it is a command to banish from your mind the opinions you have held about property, your feeling for it, your excessive desire for it, your feverish worries about it, all the cares which like thorns torment human existence and choke the seed of life. There is nothing great and enviable in merely being without property, considered in itself and apart from finding life. If there were, then those who have nothing at all, the helpless who beg for their bread, the paupers thrown on to the roads, would, though ignorant of God and his righteousness, be more blessed and dear to God than all others and alone have a hold on eternal life merely by being destitute of the most elementary necessities' (*Quis dives salvetur?*, 11).

The communism of property practised at first in Jerusalem was only an application of the communism of love which Jesus enjoined on his disciples and to which his recommendation to sell their possessions for the benefit of the needy was an emphatic exhortation. To see in primitive Christianity a movement of social revolution centred on the question of property is plainly mistaken. At first there was no intention of changing the social order; but the communism of love, as the principle for everybody, carried within it the seeds of social change. The disciples, even the Twelve, had to learn by experience how to apply it in practice. The most that can be said about the first Christians is that their belief was, as the letter of James puts it, that God had 'chosen those who are poor in the eyes of the world to be rich in faith and to inherit the kingdom promised to those who love him' (James 2.5). God had done so not because poverty in itself was more pleasing to him than riches, but because among the poor many had learned to believe in Jesus Christ, whereas the rich for the most part had been too self-satisfied to accept and follow him.

Private property in some measure was found to be necessary, but seductive. Paul had to take his Corinthian converts sharply to task for selfishness and snobbery. Even at the *agape*, the common meal taken together in conjunction with the Eucharist as a manifestation of fellowship, some who were better off sat apart and hurriedly ate the food they brought with them so as not to have to share it with the poor, who went hungry (1 Cor 11.17-22. Cf. *The Theology of St Paul*, by F. Prat, 5th imp., London 1945, Vol. I, p. 122). James too found snobbery in the Church. He scolded those who toadied to the rich and slighted the poor, even at worship in Jerusalem, as offending grievously against Christ's law of love: 'If you show snobbery, you are committing a sin and you stand convicted as transgressors by that Law' (James 2.1-4, 8-10).

Thus frank social criticism learnt from Jesus was maintained within the Christian community. Not yet did it range beyond. Only within the Christian community, unhampered by past history and ulterior motives, could expression be given to the principles of brotherly love and correction. In consequence a certain ambivalence appears in the early Christian attitude to such features of the existing social order as slavery. This is discernible in Paul's letters. On the one hand, he stresses the equality of the baptized: 'There is no such thing as Jew and Greek, slave and freeman, male and female; you are all one person in Christ Jesus' (Gal 3.28). On the other, he counsels slaves to obey their masters 'out of reverence for the Lord' (Col 3.22).

The full idea of social equality and freedom fell outside the perspective of Peter, Paul, James and anyone else in the early Church. There is no hint in the New Testament that Christians shared our horror of slavery or felt the need to denounce it. They took it for granted. It was a universal institution built into the fabric of society and in large measure the basis of its economy. Their concern was to proclaim the Gospel and correct what fell short of it in their own communities. The immediate effect of preachers and writers was not to provoke a social revolution but to inspire an ideal of human relations which neutralised social distinctions among Christians. This is well illustrated in Paul's letter to Philemon about his runaway slave, Onesimus, who had joined Paul and become a Christian. Philemon is to welcome Onesimus back 'no longer as a slave, but as more than a slave: as a dear brother, very dear to me and how much dearer to you, both as a man and as a Christian' (Philem 16). It is possible that Paul is hinting that Philemon should emancipate his slave.

The interpretation of 1 Corinthians 7.20-21 is disputed. The New English Bible translates: 'Every man should remain in the condition in which he was called. Were you a slave when you were called? Do not let that trouble you; but if the chance of liberty should come, take it'. At any rate Paul is not recommending social passivity but a true sense of values. Besides, if Christian preachers were to remain free to proclaim the Gospel, it was necessary for them not to give colour to the suspicion of the civil authorities that they were fomenting social unrest. And if they were to have the proper effect it was important that they should not encourage the newly converted to associate the gift of faith with temporal advantage.

Christian tolerance of slavery must be judged in its historical context. Seneca, Roman statesman and Stoic philosopher of the first Christian century, attacked the inhumanity with which most masters treated their slaves. 'They are slaves, people exclaim. No, they are human beings. Slaves! No, unpretentious friends. Slaves! Well, fellow-slaves, if one reflects that Fortune has equal rights over slaves and free men alike. That is why I smile at those who think it degrading for a man to dine with his slaves. It is only because the etiquette of pride surrounds the householder that the troop of slaves standing by at dinner has to keep silent throughout the meal... I pass over other instances of cruel, inhuman conduct towards slaves. We treat them as beasts of burden, never as men' (Ep. 47.1-5). Yet not even Seneca set about instigating a movement of wholesale emancipation. The Church's tolerance of slavery will be considered more fully in the final chapter.

The exhortations to obedience addressed by Peter and Paul to wives, the young and slaves suggest that in the Christian communities the idea of emancipation was in the air (1 Pet 2.18; 3.1-7; Eph 5.22, 24; Col 3.18; Tit 2.5). Both recognize that the Christian vocation is one of liberty, but are concerned lest liberty turn into licence, 'a screen for wrongdoing' (Gal 5.13; 1 Pet 2.16). Paul, champion of Christian freedom from the bonds of the Jewish law, is especially anxious that his teaching should not be made an excuse for unseemly behaviour on the part of women. His exhortations on this subject have earned for him a reputation in some quarters for antifeminism. It has, however, to be remembered that his letters were addressed to Christian men and women living in the Hellenistic world where moral standards, especially in matters of sex, were notoriously lax. Even in 'advanced' Corinth it would have been regarded as shockingly daring for a woman to address a public gathering, and Paul shared Peter's concern that the behaviour of Christians should be 'such as even pagans can recognise as good' (1 Pet 2.12).

The overall impression which the New Testament gives us of the status of women in the first years is certainly not that they were merely passive members of the Christian community. Nothing in what they wrote suggests that Paul, Peter, James, John and Jude thought that they ought to be. So far from being unduly conservative, Paul provoked the first great controversy in the Church by his insistence on the liberty of the Gospel.

The first Christians were Jews for whom to believe in Jesus Christ did not mean to forsake 'the Law and the prophets' but to come to know the reality prefigured therein and to observe its prescriptions according to the spirit and not the letter, as Jesus had done and taught them to do. But once the Church moved out into the Hellenistic world and began to convert Greek people the question arose whether they too should keep the Mosaic Law. Paul, though a Jew brought up in the strict tradition of the Pharisees and trained in the Rabbinic schools of Jerusalem, held out against it. His insistence on freedom for the Gentile Christians was matched by the insistence of the Judaizers on their obligation, and the Christian Church experienced its first internal crisis.

The dispute led to the convoking of the first council of the Church in Jerusalem (Acts 15.1-29). The decision was in favour of liberty, and a decree to that effect was sent out to all the communities with the significant words: 'It is the decision of the Holy Spirit, and our decision. . .' For our enquiry the manner of reaching the decision is as important as the decision itself. It provides clear evidence of the way in which the Church, in the belief of the apostolic age, is guided by the Holy Spirit and comes to a fuller understanding of the Gospel through a process of doctrinal controversy, debate and, finally, authoritative decision.

Had the Christians in Jerusalem been content to keep to themselves, nobody would have interfered with them. But as they spoke out openly of Jesus Christ and their message contained incisive criticism of the authorities for having rejected and put to death him whom the prophets foretold, public notice was taken. Their preaching aroused hostility in Jerusalem which mounted in intensity until it broke into active persecution.

43

It is important to note that right from the beginning the proclamation of the Gospel led to conflict with the state. The account of his trial before Pilate and the official notice posted to his cross show plainly that Jesus was executed by the civil authorities on a charge of subversion against the state (Lk 23.1-5; Jn 19.19-22). The activity of the apostles after Pentecost met with like opposition from the Jewish ruling council. Peter and John were arrested and charged with a breach of the peace. They defended their conduct in memorable words which define in principle the limits of Christian obedience to secular rulers: 'Is it right in God's eyes for us to obey you rather than God? Judge for yourselves. We cannot possibly give up speaking of the things we have seen and heard' (Acts 4.8-20. Cf. *Roman Society and Roman Law in the New Testament*, by A. N. Sherwin-White, Oxford 1963). As the Church moved outwards it came more directly up against the sovereignty of Rome.

The Roman Empire had two faces. Corresponding to them two distinct attitudes of Christians to the state are discernible in the New Testament writings. The first is formulated by Paul in his letter to the Romans. The second appears in the book of Revelation. Both are pertinent to our enquiry and must be examined closely.

Paul writes: 'Every person must submit to the supreme authorities. There is no authority but by the act of God, and the existing authorities are instituted by him; consequently, anyone who rebels against authority is resisting a divine institution, and those who resist have themselves to blame for the punishment they will receive' (Rom 13.1-2).

Taken in isolation these words appear to advocate uncritical and unconditional obedience to the civil authorities, and have sometimes been taken or cited in that sense. But that cannot be what is intended. It would contradict what Jesus taught by word and example, and would be irreconcilable with Paul's own general estimate of secular rulers and his practice in regard to their demands.

Paul had no exalted opinion of civil authorities, Roman or Jewish. For him they lacked the only wisdom that really matters, the wisdom which comes from God: 'The powers that rule the world have never known it; for if they had, they would not have crucified the Lord of glory' (1 Cor 2.6-8). By the rulers of the world Paul certainly means human rulers. Probably he also means the invisible demonic powers which, in Jewish and Christian belief of the time, are active in all earthly happenings, using human beings as their effective agents. Even so, it is the wisdom of visible political rulers which he is calling in question. Therefore he would not have Christians refer disputes among themselves to the civil courts for arbitration. They should be settled within the Christian community (1 Cor 6.2).

What then do Paul's words to the Romans mean? Certainly not that the proper Christian attitude to the state is one of uncritical, servile submission. He was writing to Christians living in Rome during the reign of Nero. Their inclination was to regard the Roman state as demonic and to think that they were absolved from all obligation to obey it. Paul was apprehensive, anxious to make it clear that they had a duty to obey when obedience was due. He had reason to be apprehensive.

In the eyes of the Roman administration and of pagan Romans generally, the refusal of Christians to take part in the emperor-cult was proof of their disloyalty to the state and of the radically anti-social nature of the Christian religion. This view is plainly reflected by the Roman historians Tacitus and Suetonius in their condemnation of Christians. Tacitus connects Nero's persecution with the great fire which devastated much of Rome in the summer of A.D. 64. He tells that Nero, to allay the persistent rumour that he had ordered the fire in order to clear a site for his building schemes, 'set up as culprits and punished with the utmost severity a class hated for their outrages, who are commonly called Christians. Christus, from whom their name is derived, was executed at the hands of the procurator Pontius Pilate in the reign of Tiberius. Checked for the moment, this pernicious superstition broke out again not only in Judaea, the source of the evil, but even in Rome, that receptacle for everything that is sordid and degrading from every quarter of the earth, which finds a following there.

Accordingly, arrests were made and on the evidence of those who confessed an immense number of Christians were convicted, not so much on the charge of arson as because of their hatred of the human race' (*Annals*, 15.44). Suetonius too had a poor opinion of the Christians. In his life of the emperor Claudius he writes, probably referring to the violent opposition of Jews to Christian preachers in Rome: 'Since the Jews were continually making disturbances at the instigation of Chrestus, Claudius expelled them from Rome' (*Vita Claudii*, 25.4; cf. Acts 18.2). And of Nero he writes: 'In his reign abuses were severely punished and repressed . . ., punishment was inflicted on the Christians, a set of men adhering to a novel and mischievous superstition' (*Vita Neronis*, 16).

The reputation of Christians at Rome, though undeserved, could not be ignored by the leaders of the Church. It seems justifiable to conclude that Paul was anxious that Christians in Rome should lend no colour to it by reluctance to give the state its due because it was based on other than Christian principles and claimed more than its due. That is how Chrysostom interpreted Romans 13: 'Paul is anxious to make it plain to all that by obeying the rulers we are not doing them a favour but carrying out our duty. In this way he tried to win over unbelieving rulers to respect for religion and believing subjects to obedience. For at that time it was commonly said, to the discredit of the apostles, that they were seditious persons planning revolution and aiming in all they said and did at subverting the established institutions' (*Hom. in Rom.*, PG 24.687c).

Light is thrown on Paul's meaning not only by the circumstances in which he wrote but also by the context in which he introduces the subject of civil obedience. The matter under discussion is the Christian law of brotherly love and its practical applications. Quite naturally the question of persecution arises, and Paul says: 'Call down blessings on your persecutors: blessings, not curses. . . . Never pay back evil for evil. If possible, in so far as it lies with you, live at peace with all men. My dear friends, do not seek revenge. . . . Do not let evil conquer you, but use good to defeat evil' (Rom 12.14,

17-19,21). Then the passage on the duty of obedience to the state follows, concluding with an exhortation: 'Discharge your obligations to all men; pay tax and toll, reverence and respect, to those to whom they are due. Leave no claim outstanding against you, except that of mutual love' (13.7-8). At this point the main theme of brotherly love is resumed.

The argument is clear. Even though the state should be totalitarian and should persecute them for refusing to give it what it has no right to demand, Christians are still bound by the law of love and must repay the evil done to them by the state with the good of obedience to it in all that it has a right to command. They must refuse the one and concede the other because whatever authority the state has is not an authority apart from God but an authority given it by God. Thus Paul commends civil obedience, but a discriminating obedience for which he gives the criterion: submit to the civil authorities in so far as they have and use authority from God to command. It is the same doctrine as Jesus taught.

Paul's aim is strictly limited. He was not writing a treatise on political philosophy but a letter to meet the requirements of a particular Christian community at a particular time. Though he enunciates principles of wide application, we must not expect to find answers to questions with which Paul was not concerned and to which he is unlikely to have given a thought. For instance the question: How do rulers get their authority from God? Has every *de facto* government authority from God? Is rebellion ever permissible? These are very important questions which Christians were to ask at a later date.

When we turn to the Book of Revelation we find that the author, traditionally identified with the apostle John, appears at first sight to contradict what Paul writes to the Romans, even when understood in a limited sense. 'Then out of the sea,' he writes, 'I saw a beast rising. . . . The dragon conferred upon it his power to rule, and great authority. The whole world went after the beast in wondering admiration. Men worshipped the beast also, and chanted: "Who is like the Beast? Who can fight against it?" The beast opened its mouth in blasphemy against God, and it was also allowed to wage war on God's people and to defeat them, and was granted authority over every tribe and people, language and nation. All on earth will worship it, except those whose names the Lamb that was slain keeps in the roll of the living' (Rev 13.1-8).

Here the writer, with his eyes on its excesses, describes the Roman Empire with its emperor-worship and totalitarian claims in the language of Semitic mythology as a beast, a minion of the dragon Satan, to which all the world has been made subject and to which men of every nation render honour and obedience.

In the form in which we have it the Book of Revelation was probably written towards the end of Domitian's reign when Christians were persecuted with especial severity. In effect what the author says is that people of the time submitted cravenly to imperial Rome, not because it had rightful authority to demand obedience but because it had the power to enforce its will. Though disguised in mythological sumbols, his reference to Rome must have been as unmistakable to Christians then as it is now. But he uses the instance of Rome to expose the demonic character of every totalitarian state and to warn Christians against submitting to its unwarranted demands. The rule of Rome he does not hesitate to identify with the dominion of Satan, in Jewish and Christian tradition the blasphemous aper of God, because the Rome of that period demanded of its subjects unconditional obedience which belongs to God alone.

Paul would not have disagreed. He shared the primitive Christian belief that until the coming of Christ the world was under the sway of demonic powers made manifest especially through human agents in high places who demand what amounts to worship (1 Cor 15.24).

In one respect the attitude of the primitive Church to the state was unreservedly positive. Because they were not permitted by the teaching of Jesus to renounce the state as an institution, yet could not submit to it unconditionally, Christians were required to pray for the civil authorities at all times, even while suffering persecution at their hands. Accordingly Paul wrote to Timothy: 'I urge you that petitions, prayers, intercessions, and thanksgivings be offered for all men; for sovereigns and all in high office, that we may lead a tranquil and quiet life in full observance of religion and high standards of morality' (1 Tim 2.1-2). The sovereign at the time was Nero!

The first Christians were by no means blind to the merits and benefits of the Roman Empire. The peace it imposed, and the roads and seaways it provided and guarded, enabled them to travel safely up and down the Mediterranean world preaching the Gospel and founding churches. Paul valued his Roman citizenship. He used its privileges for the benefit of the Gospel, and in lodging an appeal to Caesar he openly acknowledged the superiority of Roman justice at its source. But the early Christians would not have been human had they not felt keenly the sting of social rejection and been tempted, especially when persecuted, to regard the Empire as an incarnation of evil. This feeling is reflected in the New Testament by such words, frequently used to designate Christians, as aliens, strangers, passing travellers, temporary lodgers, and the like (e.g. Eph 2.19; Heb 11.13; 1 Pet 1.1; 2.11).

Thus the attitude of the first Christians to the state was as complex as Jesus' attitude. In it was a tension between the duty to obey and the duty to judge which was not resolved through the centuries. Tacitus doubtless spoke for most Roman intellectuals and civil servants when he branded Christians as haters of humanity; but such a condemnation of a religious group inspired by the ideal of universal brotherhood is intelligible only if we see in it an accusation not of misanthropy but of nonconformity. Prechristian antiquity knew of only one sovereignty, the sovereignty of the state, and imperial Rome was a totalitarian state. Christians were unable to accept and submit to its absolutism, and persecution inevitably followed.

It did not help matters that persecution had the effect, as it is wont to do, of driving its victims to extremes of antagonism. Literary expression of it in the first century is to be found in the Book of Revelation, as we have seen. In the second century it appears in the writing of Hippolytus (A.D. 170-236), the first Christian exegete, who maintains that the proper attitude to the state for Christians is a combination of total repudiation and patient endurance of it as a 'trial' permitted by God (*In Dan.*, 4.9). This, however, was only one side of the Christian response to the state and society in the first centuries, the side which filled Romans like Tacitus with revulsion.

The other side appears in Tertullian (A.D. 160-220), a contemporary of Hippolytus. Defending Christians against the charge of being anti-social, he writes: 'We are not Brahmins or naked fakirs of India or men of the woods or escapists from life. We are mindful that we owe gratitude to God, the Lord and Creator, and reject none of the fruits of his work. We simply school ourselves not to use them to excess or amiss. We do not renounce your forum, your meatmarket, your baths, your shops, your factories, your taverns, your weekly fairs, or any part of your trade and commerce. On the contrary, we share your lives as far as this world is concerned. We go to sea with you, serve in the army with you, spend our holidays and go out shopping like you. We add our skill to yours and openly offer our services for your employment' (*Apologia*, 42.1-3).

The same point was made less rhetorically some time before by the unknown author of the Letter to Diognetus. Christians, he says, are not distinguishable from other people by country, language, customs and habits of life, yet 'they show forth the remarkable and admittedly strange order of their own citizenship' (*Epistle to Diognetus*, 5. Trans. H.G. Meecham, Manchester 1949).

The real objection to Christianity felt by imperial Rome was in part this claim to a citizenship higher than that of Rome, and in part the claim it made to show the way of salvation even to the Roman world. For, as Celsus, a late second-century Platonist writer, put it: 'Christianity is a rite of foreign and barbarous origin. The apostles were worthless individuals, tax-gatherers and low-class sailors' (Origen, *Contra Celsum*, 1.65). It was insulting to Romans to suggest that they should look to Judaea for salvation and associate themselves with the rabble which made up the Christian brotherhood.

Chapter 4.

CHURCH AND STATE AFTER CONSTANTINE

A.D. 313 marks a turning-point in Christian history and social thought. In that year the emperor Constantine and his colleague Licinius decreed religious toleration for the whole Roman Empire, and from being an unlawful and persecuted sect Christianity became first a licensed cult and then a state religion. But, as Christians soon discovered, the problem of the relation of Church and state was not so much resolved as transposed.

St Paul had recommended his converts not to be anxious about the affairs of this world: not to pine for emancipation if they were slaves; not to seek separation if they were married or marriage if they were single; not to be preoccupied with buying and selling if they were engaged in commerce, as at Corinth; for 'the whole frame of this world is passing away' (1 Cor 7.20-31). During the first three centuries the stress of Christian preaching continued to be on detachment from the affairs of the world. There was neither incentive nor opportunity for Christians to take part in public life and to concern themselves with the improvement of the social order. Even to have suggested it would have confirmed the suspicions of the state that they were seditious at heart.

In his defence of Christians against the charge of seditious intent Tertullian, with typical exaggeration, denied that they had any interest at all in the concerns of this world: 'No affairs are so alien to us as public affairs. We know only of one commonwealth, which is not of this world. . . Our interest in this world is to get out of it as quickly as possible' (*Apol*, 2.38.3; 41.15). As we have seen, Tertullian gave in the same work a very different account of the attitude of Christians in his defence against the charge that they were anti-social, stressing the extent to which they shared in the life of the Empire. His inconsistency reflects the ambiguity in the Christian attitude to the state during the years of persecution. They were unable to repudiate its authority altogether or to accept it without question.

After emancipation close association with the state did not bring only embarrassment. Imperial patronage enabled the Church to influence the moral outlook of society directly. Its influence was felt, but only gradually. For a long time after 313 most of the population of the Roman world remained outside the Church, and of the numbers who streamed in many had mixed motives and little instruction, so that a struggle ensued against laxity within and low moral standards outside the Christian communities. Besides, the moral perceptions of even the best Christians were in some important respects defective or undeveloped. A case in point is their view of slavery.

Christianity was born into a world long since firmly established on slavery. Christians accepted the situation but never took it simply for granted. As we have seen, the Church of the New Testament did not condemn slavery but sought to imbue masters and slaves with the new spirit of brotherhood. During the years of persecution masters and slaves shared as equals the same sacraments and the same sufferings, and sometimes went to martyrdom together. The absolute religious equality proclaimed and practised by Christians was a novelty which the Roman Empire looked at askance. It was a negation of the existing social order and especially of the institution of slavery itself. After emancipation the Church exerted a steady pressure for the improvement of the condition of individual slaves, the effects of which are discernible in the many mitigations introduced by imperial legislation from the time of Constantine and especially under Justinian, who in the sixth century reformed the Roman legal code. Henceforth, to give one example, slaves gained their freedom when, with the consent of their masters, they became priests and when, even without their consent, they entered one of the religious groups of monks which were springing up at that time.

In their theory as well as their practice Christians were evidently uneasy about slavery even while they sought to justify the institution. Their theologians rejected the view of ancient philosophers like Aristotle that it was founded on nature and justifiable on that account. Augustine saw it as a condition of life consequent upon the Fall, the result of original sin (*De Civ. Dei*, 19,5,16). Gregory of Nyssa rejected it outright (*Hom. in Eccles*, 4). John Chrysostom repeatedly held up to his congregations the ideal of a Christian society in which there would be no slaves but only free workers (*Les Esclaves Chrétiens depuis les premiers temps de la Domination Romaine en Occident*, by Paul Allard, Paris 1900, pp. 416-33). Jerome attests that in his day clerics of slave origin were numerous (Ep. 18). At least one of the early popes had been a slave: Callistus in the third century. In its assemblies the Church took no account of the social condition of the faithful, and it encouraged masters to free their slaves gratuitously as an act of charity (Allard, *ibid.*). Against Roman practice and law the Church recognized the matrimonial unions of Christian slaves as legitimate marriages and condemned masters who took the wives of their slaves to bed as adulterers (Allard, *ibid.*).

Unfortunately, because of his eminence as a Christian thinker, Augustine's theoretical justification of slavery as a penalty for sin won general acceptance, an acceptance which in the course of the centuries was perpetuated more because his argument was thought to be supported by Catholic tradition than because it was confirmed by critical examination. His argument is invalid. From the premise that slavery is the result of human sin it follows not that it is morally acceptable, a penalty which is just because imposed by God and apportioned to men's deserts, but that it is morally objectionable, a result as bad as its human causes. The doctrine of original sin teaches only that all men are in a sense slaves of sinfulness: it gives no justification whatever for the enslavement of people but stresses the perversity of men as they are. The most that Augustine might have claimed in justification of the institution of slavery is that in his day it was a lesser evil than the total breakdown of social order in which a sudden universal abolition would have resulted.

A problem for the Christian conscience more acutely felt

was that posed by military service and war in defence of the Roman Empire. War must always pose a problem for Christians, because the law of love includes love of enemies and enjoins patient endurance of aggressors without retaliation. Taken literally, Christ's exhortation to turn the other cheek and to hand over one's cloak as well to him who steals one's coat seems to rule out all resort to violent resistance (Mt 5.38-42; 11.29-30). For Christians before 313 there was also the further objection to military service that it meant taking an oath of unconditional service to the emperor, fighting for a pagan and persecuting state, and celebrating victory by assisting at ceremonies and sacrifices in honour of false gods. For these reasons some early Church writers condemned Christians who engaged in military service. That many evaded it on grounds of conscience is clear from Origen's defence of Christians against the charge of lack of patriotism (*Contra Celsum*, 13.73-5). Many others, however, served in the imperial armies, sometimes with distinction. Christian opinion was divided on the issue, and no clear directive was given by Church authorities.

Nevertheless, as long as the state definitely opposed the Church, the problem for the Christian conscience which the relation between Church and state raised was comparatively simple. Christians could have no doubt where their duty lay: to apply the Gospel to their own lives and learn to love those who hated them. They then had every excuse for regarding themselves as pilgrims passing through a foreign country, enduring the obstacles put in their path by the state and hoping for toleration in return for social quiescence. Such was, and always is, the Christian predicament under a totalitarian state, and the advantage for the Christian conscience.

As soon as the state renounced its totalitarian claims by acknowledging the autonomy of the Church in the spiritual sphere, an entirely new situation arose in which not only the prospect but also the problem for Christians was radically altered.

Understandably, the reaction of Christians to the un-expected change in their status and prospects was at first one

56

of unalloyed thankfulness to God and to Constantine. Their whole attitude to the state and cooperation with it changed. For instance, at the first synod of bishops after emancipation, held at Arles in 314, military service was declared to be lawful (Canon 3). And Eusebius, the first historian of the Church, saw now in the unification of the world and the peace established by the Roman Empire a divinely guided preparation for the spreading of the Gospel (*De Laudibus Constantini*, 3.5). But within a short time the Church had a foretaste of what its changed relation to the state would mean for its freedom of action.

A dispute arose in the Church about the validity of orders conferred by bishops who had apostatized during the last great persecution ten years before under the emperors Diocletian and Maximilian. Basically this was a theological controversy and therefore a Church affair. But as it led to civil disorder it also involved the state, and Constantine intervened. Constantine was not, however, content to restore public order but took it upon himself to settle the dispute which had disturbed it. He first summoned Church councils and then, when they failed to produce agreement and peace in the Church, he made himself the arbiter, hearing both parties and deciding the issue. He came to the same conclusion as the pope and most of the bishops, that the orders of apostates remained valid, and by imperial decree he suppressed the Donatist party which held the contrary view.

The result was satisfactory for the Church as a whole, but the manner of reaching it set an ominous precedent. At such a time and under such an emperor it was perhaps impossible for the pope and bishops to resist interference by the state or even to suspect the danger of acquiescence. Yet in letting it go without demur they in effect encouraged interference by the state in Church affairs and sowed the seeds of centuries of conflict. From that date the state began to assume the role of patron of the Church and to consider its affairs as part of its own responsibility.

In the East the Church, living under the shadow of the new imperial capital of Constantinople, became a department of the state. In the West, centred on the old Rome, it refused to accept subordination and came to make a counter-claim. Against the contention of Constantine's successor, Constantius, that his will should be taken as law in the Church as well as in the state (Athanasius, *Hist. Arian.*, 34), its champions in the West argued that as a Christian the emperor was subject no less than any other of the faithful to the law and discipline of the divinely instituted Church (Cf. C.N. Cochrane, *Christianity and Classical Culture*, London 1944, p. 187).

The importance of these events for our enquiry is that they mark the beginning of an era in which the distinction between Church and state and their spheres of responsibility became confused. Experience showed that religious toleration and imperial benevolence did not solve the problem of the relation between the two. Pope and emperor saw it differently. What we can see is the growth of a new tension between Church and state and a tendency in each to claim jurisdiction over the other.

Up to this time no sustained effort had been made to work out a Christian theory of their proper relation. It had not been prompted or assisted either by the sacred scriptures inherited from the Jews or by the philosophy taken over from the Greeks; for each in its own way knew of only one sovereignty. Not until their emancipation had Christians been faced with the problem of living under two sovereignties, each with a legitimate claim on them. What the conflict of the fourth and fifth centuries did was to bring the problem into focus and to stimulate Christian thinking about it. The need led to the speculation, at once theological and political, of Augustine (350-430) and Gelasius (pope 492-496).

There was never any doubt in Christian thought accepted by the church as a whole that political society is good in itself. But it was equally clear that the relation between rulers and ruled, masters and servants, had been corrupted by the sinfulness of men. Instead of the fraternity, concord and liberty intended by God there was oppression, rebellion and slavery. This corruption was an outgrowth of 'original sin', the alienation of man from God and consequently of man from man, symbolized in the biblical account of the Fall of Man. For the sickness of society as for the sinfulness of man Christ had brought the remedy. At the political level the remedy lay in distinguishing between the kingdom of God and the kingdom of men, and in seeking the kingdom of God first, as Christ taught. Thus far Christians were agreed. Where they differed was in the measure in which they equated the kingdom of God with the visible Church.

Augustine allowed no simple identification between the two. Distinguishing between 'the city of God' and 'the city of man', he wrote: 'The two cities are made by two loves, the earthly by the love of self leading to contempt of God, and the heavenly by love of God leading to contempt of self. The one glories in itself, the other in God. The one seeks glory from men; to the other the greatest glory is the witness of God in conscience' (*De Civitate Dei*, 14.28). Augustine did not accept that the church is without reservation the city of God or that the state is simply the city of man. 'Just as what is of the devil inside the fold must be convicted, so what is of Christ outside must be recognized' (*De Baptismo*, 4.14). For him the visible Church and the state are both necessary means to an end outside themselves which is ultimately the salvation of men willed by God. Each is concerned with peace: the state with exterior peace, resulting from the suppression of strife and the provision of the conditions necessary for earthly existence; the Church with interior peace, springing from right relationship with God and men. As the function of the Church is higher, so in a sense the state must serve the interests of the Church, but only in so far as the Church in turn serves and represents the kingdom of God.

Having made these careful distinctions, Augustine could write: 'How blessed would emperors be if they put their power at the service of the Divine Majesty with a view to spreading Christianity' (*De Civ. Dei*, 5.24). Regrettably, those who in later times appealed to Augustine's authority, and to these words in particular, in support of the intervention of the Church in the affairs of the state paid no heed to his distinctions. What he stressed was the primacy of the spiritual order, not the subordination of the state to the Church.

A somewhat different view of Church-state relations, which became the classical theory for many centuries, was expressed by Pope Gelasius I. It appears in a letter of 494 to the eastern emperor Anastasius protesting against the support the latter was giving to the heretical and schismatical tendencies of the Patriarch of Constantinople. Before the time of Christ, Gelasius wrote, kings were also priests and all authority, religious as well as civil, was concentrated in their hands. So the state became despotic and oppressive. When Christ came, being mindful of human weakness and the evils of pride, he separated the two functions, assigning to each its proper task and dignity. Since then the fullness of authority belongs to none but Christ; for he alone, being God and perfect man without any tendency to sin, is able to wield absolute power aright. Thus the distinction between Church and state, and their spheres of action, is a consequence of the coming of Christ and a condition laid down by him for the salvation of mankind. Yet of the two the spiritual is comparatively the higher since it is concerned with the souls of men, including rulers (Ep. 8; *De Anathematis Vinculo*, 11; PL 59.42,108-9).

The merit of the Gelasian formula is that it recognizes the necessity of distinguishing between the spheres of responsibility of Church and state, and the evils for human welfare of confusing them. Its weakness is that it fails to indicate the limits of each clearly or to provide a norm for decision in cases of dispute. Its ambiguity allowed both papalists and imperialists in later times to appeal to it in support of conflicting claims, with the result that it contributed to the confusion which it sought to remove.

Before the Middle Ages no definite claim was made by the Church to have authority over the state, except in the spiritual sphere. Even Pope Gregory the Great, who may be considered the founder of the papal monarchy, made no such claim. True, he wrote to the Byzantine emperor Maurice in 593: 'Power over all men has been given to my Lords for them to open more widely the way that leads to heaven in order that the earthly kingdom may be at the service of the heavenly kingdom.' But that he meant only to echo Augustine is clear from his action. The emperor had forbidden monasteries to admit soldiers of the imperial army as monks. Gregory pointed out that the order violated conscience, but passed it on. He believed that in doing so he was not making the Church too compliant to the state but was doing his duty to both: 'Thus on both sides I have done what is due, since I recommended obedience to the emperor and did not keep silent about what I felt due to God' (Ep. 1.3.61).

It was rather the state which set itself over the Church. This was especially the case in the East. The emperor Justinian, although an orthodox and zealous Catholic, saw himself as having authority from God over spiritual as well as temporal affairs. In the preamble to a decree of 535, dealing with the conferring of orders and the upkeep of churches, he sketched the ideal of a Christian commonwealth. He made a distinction between Church and state, but in the form of a distinction between the clerical and the lay elements of a Christian society: 'The greatest gifts given by God to men are the priesthood and the imperial authority, the former for the ordering of divine things, the latter for that of human affairs. . . There is nothing to which the emperors attach more importance than the wellbeing of the clergy . . . and the truth of the doctrine they teach. If the priesthood is free from vice and full of faith in God, and if the imperial authority governs the commonwealth committed to its charge with justice and efficiency, there will be perfect harmony well able to furnish whatever is beneficial to the human race' (*Church and State through the Centuries: a Collection of Illustrative Documents*, ed. and trans. S.Z. Ehler and J.B. Morrall, London 1954, p.10). Pope and bishops are included in the commonwealth, but as part of a system presided over by the emperor.

'Caesaropapism', the tendency of the state to preside over the Church, took root in the East. In the West the opposite tendency grew, partly in reaction against the encroachment of the state, partly as a result of the feudal structure of society since the Dark Ages and the position of the bishops within it. By the Middle Ages, it could be said, the Church no longer existed in the state: the state existed in the Church.

The dominant position of the Church was not initially sought or ever complete. The popes became kings of central Italy and the bishops princes elsewhere not for theoretical reasons but in response to practical social needs. In the chaos which followed the collapse of the Empire in the West under the impact of the barbarian invasions, they were the only experienced administrators left who were willing to cooperate with the rough Germanic chieftains in restoring something of the old order and in carrying on civil government. In gratitude the new overlords endowed the Church generously with land, and in a turbulent world ownership of land gave the Church economic security and a guarantee of rights and liberties which under Germanic feudalism were tied to the land. The Church gained independence, but at heavy cost. As feudal landlords, the popes and bishops were entangled in temporal affairs and had to play two often incompatible roles. The feudal kings and princes, in return for their protection and benefactions, claimed and exercised the right of appointing bishops in their own domains and of having a voice in papal elections. More often than not they chose men whose main qualification for ecclesiastical office was their loyalty to their royal sponsors, and whose chief interest in holding it was its wealth, power and prestige. In consequence the Church suffered a serious decline in spiritual health and came under the effective control of political rulers.

Pope Gregory VII, elected in 1073, set out to free and reform the Church, and ended by propounding a new theory of its relation to the state. He condemned the practice of lay investiture and its attendant evils, reaffirmed the primatial authority of the papacy, and threatened with excommunication anyone who attempted to interfere with the freedom of papal elections. When the emperor Henry IV refused to comply, Gregory excommunicated him and freed his subjects from their oath of allegiance. In effect the pope deposed the emperor. This was a revolutionary action, effective at the time but momentous for the future. It introduced a new era in which the Church was no longer content to defend its independence against state encroachment but sought to exercise a political hegemony over Christendom.

Gregory might have justified his policy on grounds of expediency. Instead he defended it as right in principle. To the synod of bishops convoked in Rome to hear his explanation he exclaimed: 'Make sure that the whole world understands that if you have authority to bind and loose in heaven, you have authority to take away and bestow on each person, according to his merits, empires, kingdoms, principalities, duchies, marquisates, counties and all the possessions of men here on earth. You have often deprived unworthy men of patriarchates, primacies, archbishoprics and bishoprics and given them to truly religious men. If then you have ability to judge in spiritual matters, what power you must have over the things of this world!' (Ehler-Morrall, pp.42-3).

Gregory's policy and its theoretical vindication became standard practice and doctrine for the medieval Church. Under Innocent III (1198-1216) the papacy reached the zenith of its power. The pope examined candidates for the imperial throne, deposed the king of England (John), and established a ring of vassal states around the papal throne in Rome. Under Boniface VIII (1294-1303) the doctrine of 'the two swords' was explicitly formulated in the Bull *Unam Sanctam* (1302). Commenting on the text 'Look, Lord, they said, we have two swords here' (Lk 22.38), he wrote: 'We are instructed by the words of the gospel that two swords (the spiritual and the temporal) are in the power of Peter. In fact, when the apostles said, 'We have two swords here' (i.e. in the Church), the Lord did not reply, 'That is too much', but 'That is enough'. He who denies that the temporal sword is in Peter's power forgets the Lord's words, 'Put it back in its sheath.' Thus both swords, the temporal as well as the spiritual, are in the power of the Church. The former is wielded on behalf of the Church, the latter by the Church: the latter by the hand of a priest, the former by the hand of a king or knight on the word and with the consent of the priest. It is indeed necessary for one sword to be under the other, and for the temporal authority to be subject to the spiritual, (Ehler-Morrale, p.91; DZ 873).

To be fair to the doctrine of the two swords, the cultural background and historical circumstances of its origin have to be kept in mind. During the long apprenticeship of the new nations of Europe following the collapse of the Roman Empire, a period when the minds of the laity were almost entirely dormant, the intellectual and moral leadership of society had to be undertaken almost single-handed by the Church in the persons of the pope and the bishops. But whatever may be said in defence of the extension of papal jurisdiction to temporal affairs in that era, there is nothing to be said in favour of the tendentious use of sacred scripture. The currency of the theory ended with the era from which it sprang, but its influence lasted longer like a hangover, confusing the issue of Church and state.

More solid in foundation and more permanent in value was medieval theory about civil authority itself. The discussion centred on its exercise and limits rather than on its origin; for people of that epoch accepted the verdict of scripture that all authority comes from God, and commonly saw in hereditary monarchy its natural embodiment. To this extent, however, the question of origin entered the discussion, that medieval thinkers took as its agreed premise the view of Cicero and Augustine that the state is the result not of mob sympathy but of rational consent: the consent of the people to a common law for the good of the whole community. From this they drew important political conclusions.

The commonest view of political authority was that the title of the ruler to command obedience depends on the manner in which he acquires authority and the manner in which he exercises it. When political power is held by usurpation the government has no authority and the citizens may with a good conscience rebel to overthrow it, provided that the likely outcome will be a better and not a worse state of affairs. And when the government, though legitimately constituted, uses its authority in the interests of a party and not of the common good, to that extent its authority ceases and the citizens may, with the same proviso, resist its unjust laws. Both are cases of tyranny. Whereas civil disobedience and rebellion may sometimes be morally permissible, tyranny can never be. The difference is that in the case of tyranny the seditious party is not the rebellious people but the tyrannical government itself, which subverts the natural purpose of the state as intended by God (Cf. St Thomas, *Summa Theologiae*, II-II.42.2; 104.6).

Aquinas favoured constitutional monarchy on the grounds that, more effectively than any other form of government, monarchy lends itself to civil unity, and that an agreed constitution provides a check on abuse of authority. Parliamentary government, a development of a later age, Aquinas did not foresee. He was inclined to identify democracy with mob rule, but something of the democratic principle is implicit in his preference for a constitution based on popular consent and allowing a measure of shared responsibility. It seemed obvious to him that such an arrangement offers the best hope of social peace, stability and welfare.

Though to the medieval mind monarchy seemed the natural form of government, analogous to God's government of creation, political absolutism was alien to it. Not the later doctrine of 'the divine right of kings' but the contemporary dictum of Henry of Bracton that 'the King is under God and the Law' expressed its theological conviction. And precisely because the king was under God, medieval thinkers regarded the state as being in a sense under the Church. Believing as Christians that man has a supernatural and not a merely temporal end, and that the Church exists to help him attain it, they thought that in the exercise of its authority the state should be under the moral guidance of the Church.

Aquinas did not give his support to the extreme theory of the subordination of the state to the Church, even though he thought of the Church as an independent society superior in dignity and authority. Living in an age of frequent conflict between Church and state, he was well aware of the problem of their harmonious cooperation; but he believed that the remedy lay in their mutual respect for each other's proper function and rights. In this he reasserted the older and sounder Christian view.

Thus the Middle Ages had much to say about the nature and limits of political authority but little to say about its source. The problem of its source (how in fact it is derived from God) became acute during the sixteenth and seventeenth centuries.

In political terms the Renaissance and the Reformation were centrifugal movements carried along by the awakening nationalism of the new nations and their aspiration to emancipate themselves from ecclesiastical paternalism and make an independent life of their own. The medieval ideal of a supranational society of all Christian peoples under the presidency of the pope was replaced by a conception of a multiplicity of completely autonomous nation states, each with its own culture, language and Church. In each the good of society became the good of the state and the authority of the ruler became absolute. To give theoretical support to royal claims to absolute authority over state and Church, the doctrine of the divine right of kings was then propounded. According to this theory the king or prince who holds the throne by right of birth receives sovereign authority directly from God and is answerable to God alone. His subjects are always bound in conscience to obey his commands, even in matters of religion.

So, acting on the slogan *cuius regio, eius religio*, both Catholic and Protestant kings and princes imposed their religion on their subjects and suppressed nonconformism ruthlessly, claiming the right to do so in virtue of their God-given authority. It then became a matter of great importance to find a genuinely Christian answer to the questions whether in such circumstances subjects may disobey and whether they may carry resistance to the length of armed rebellion and tyrannicide.

In the controversy which ensued both views were defended by illustrious champions: King James I of England upholding the right of rulers to demand obedience in all circumstances, and Cardinal Bellarmine arguing in favour of the right of subjects to resist tyranny. By implication each gave an answer to the question how political authority is derived from God. For the divine right of kings presupposes that authority comes directly from God, whereas the right of subjects to resist is best defended on the supposition that rulers get their authority indirectly, through the consent of the people.

In parenthesis it must be said that Bellarmine's theory, held also by Suarez, differs fundamentally from the theory of Hobbes and Rousseau. For Bellarmine and Suarez society is not of conventional but of natural origin. and political authority comes not from the people but from God, though indirectly through constitutional agreement.

Neither the view that political authority comes directly from God, nor the view that it comes from him only indirectly, was altogether new, except in the use James made of the one to defend royal absolutism and Bellarmine made of the other to oppose it. Of the two Bellarmine's view, which was also urged by the Huguenots against the absolutism of the French monarchy, was the more traditional, being closer to the thought and practice of the Middle Ages than the doctrine of the divine right of kings and its tendency to totalitarianism which came into prominence in the sixteenth century.

Bellarmine's importance for our enquiry is that he went beyond the point which medieval discussion of political authority reached, and answered the question of its derivation. Aquinas had argued that in receiving his authority from God the ruler acquires a trust to fulfil, and concluded that, when the ruler oversteps the limits intended by God, his subjects have a moral right to resist and rebel because he then abuses his trust. Bellarmine agreed, but went on to the further conclusion that, this being so, political authority must be seen to come from God through the consent of the community. This conclusion was not explicitly drawn before the events of the sixteenth century posed the problem of the acquisition of civil authority more clearly and urgently than ever before.

Unlike the doctrine of the divine right of kings, Bellarmine's view has the merit of according with the evidence of history and with the main tradition of Christian theology. Hereditary monarchy in fact continued to be a viable form of government and to be regarded as 'natural' as long as it was accepted by the community. It may therefore be said to have been government by implicit consent. So to describe it is not just to play with words; for it is a fact that progressively, as one section of the community after another became dissatisfied with the system of government, it made political demands, manifesting thereby withdrawal of consent. In England, for example, the barons combined to limit the royal power; the burghers joined together to wrest a measure of freedom for their city; then, after the power of the king and the power of the ruling obligarchy were in turn limited, the commons woke up and demanded a voice in the affairs of the state.

However little the development of government by explicit consent of the governed may have had the approval and support of churchmen at the time, it merited both as being in line with Christian doctrine. For if men, created by God, are by nature free, intelligent and social, and are by grace destined to the society of God in heaven and assisted on earth to prepare for it by perfecting themselves in concert with one another, then the social order must be such as to furnish the conditions needed for their proper development both as individuals and as citizens on the way to their everlasting city. And just as no man can grow into a good man and a good citizen except by his own consent and cooperation, so the political order and government of society must be such as to win the consent and cooperation of the people.

These ideas were in the air of the sixteenth century, generated in reaction to the political absolutism and religious intolerance of the rulers of Europe. They were not entirely novel but grew out of the notion, deep in Christian thought and traceable to Jesus' own teaching, that political power should depend on moral forces inherent in the community and be used in the service of the community.

Nevertheless, Bellarmine defended the papal 'right' to depose tyrannical emperors and princes. This conclusion did not follow from his argument but resulted from a failure to recognise that the right claimed by some of the popes had at best a temporary validity. In an era when the political order of Europe was adolescent and in need of tutelage which only the

Church could provide, no institution existed and no means could be found for getting rid of a tyrant apart from the papacy. Bellarmine failed to foresee that as the political order grew up it would develop the means of managing its own affairs. His own argument should have prepared him for this development. For if political authority was to be seen as deriving from God through popular consent, and if the people might withdraw their consent legitimately in the interests of the common good, it was to be expected that as they reached political maturity they would develop civil institutions needed to control civil authority and correct its abuse.

The political theory of Bellarmine and Suarez failed to win wide acceptance and did not receive official approval until a much later date. In an era of revolutionary change in Europe which produced first the religious schism of the Reformation, then the religious scepticism of the Enlightenment, and finally the secularisation of society in the Revolution, the minds of Catholics, preoccupied with defence of the Church, were ill disposed to new ideas and liberal views. Moreover, Bellarmine's argument was thought to prove too much. For if popular consent was the source under God of the authority of emperors and kings, it was likewise the source of the sovereignty of popes over the Papal States. This conclusion the ecclesiastical hierarchy was unwilling to admit because it assumed that the temporal power of the papacy was indispensable to the independence of the church and as such had a higher validity.

Had Bellarmine and Suarez won a favourable hearing, their doctrine might have saved the Catholic Church from being identified with the *ancien régime* which the revolutionaries sought to sweep away, and would have enabled it to play a positive part in the making of the modern world. Instead, the Catholic Church leant heavily on the old Catholic monarchies even while they endeavoured to use it for their own mundane purposes; and the conservatism of the papacy, itself the oldest monarchy and absolutist in rule, blinded the hierarchy to what was good in the aims of the Revolution. Liberty, equality and fraternity, popular government, and radical reconstruction of the social order accordingly, so far from being contrary to the spirit of the Gospel, are rather in harmony with it.

Unfortunately the revolutionaries did not practise what they preached and were opposed not only to the temporal but also to the spiritual authority of the Church. It was their practice which alienated Catholics. The popes opposed separation of Church and state because they feared that it would lead, not to 'a free Church in a free state', but to the domination of the Church by the state. What happened in France confirmed their fears. If Pope Pius IX went further than his predecessors in condemning 'progress, liberalism and modern civilisation' (*Syllabus of Errors*, 1864), it was because his efforts to achieve a reconciliation between the Catholic Church and the Revolution had gone further and had conspicuously failed. Regrettably, the papacy did not look beyond the confines of continental Europe to Great Britain and the United States of America—where Catholic experience of liberalism was very different—and allowed its preoccupation with the Papal States to determine its judgement.

A more judicious and favourable appraisal was made in England, where liberalism was native and liberals were really liberal, by John Henry Newman, one of the most penetrating minds of the day. No theologian of the nineteenth century had studied the intellectual movements of the age more closely or was better equipped to pass a balanced judgement on them.

Newman opposed only liberalism in religion, 'the doctrine that there is no truth in religion, but that one creed is as good as another'. But he favoured religious toleration on the grounds that in a country like Britain, where many sects exist side by side, it is a practical necessity, and that in the modern world, where people are no longer disposed to accept a religion because it is traditional or is imposed by their rulers, it is better in principle. He argued that at a time like the present, when society is developed and its members are eager and able to take an active part in its management, it is right that people should be free to choose their religion in the light of their conscience and that the state should be religiously neutral.

Whatever may have been suitable in the past, in the modern world the separation of Church and state is desirable.

Newman recognised that there is much that is true and good in the theory of liberal democracy, especially in the value it puts on the personality and responsibility of the individual, the fundamental equality of men, and government by consent of the governed. But he also saw a danger of a general decline into mediocracy in its stress on equality, and a danger of foolish policies and ventures being adopted in response to popular clamour. What above all worried him was the shallow optimism of so many liberals who shared Rousseau's romantic conception of human nature and were blind to the fact of 'original sin' and to the need of divine grace and unremitting moral effort.

In short, Newman accepted the ideal of democracy as being close to Christianity, and was convinced that democratic practice is inevitable and desirable in the modern world. But at the same time he saw clearly that democracy, far from being a sure guarantee of personal liberty and the pursuit of excellence, can endanger both. Despite the danger, however, he thought that 'nothing great or living can be done except when men are self-governing and independent' (*Political Thought of John Henry Newman*, by T. Kenny, London 1958, p. 182). The safeguard he saw in a deep sense of tradition, understood not as a mere attachment to ideas and institutions handed down from the past, but as something living and growing. 'Tradition', he wrote, 'in its fullness is necessarily unwritten; it is the mode in which a society has felt and acted during a certain period, and it cannot be circumscribed any more than a man's countenance and manner can be conveyed to strangers in a set of propositions' (*Via Media*, Vol. 1, London 1918, p. 32).

The importance of Newman's views is not that they put him in the front rank of political thinkers alongside men like John Stuart Mill, but that they were the views of a great theologian whose life spanned the nineteenth century and whose reflections on the problem of Christianity in the modern world led him to accept much that popes and bishops of the time opposed and which later popes and bishops were to recommend. He picked up and carried forward the line of Christian political thought running through Aquinas, Bellarmine and Suarez which had been lost to sight in the dust of conflict raised by the age of Revolution.

When Pope Pius IX died in 1878 Rome and most Catholics in Europe were at odds with the world. Society had changed, but not the Church. For three-quarters of a century popes and bishops had spent their energies combatting liberalism in the belief that it was a threat to Christianity and in the hope that it was only a temporary aberration. This failure on the part of its hierarchy to grasp that in one form or another liberalism had come to stay, and the support it gave to anti-liberal regimes in Europe, had unfortunate results for the Catholic Church. In Catholic countries, and not least in the Papal States, many among the educated and professional class became alienated and hostile.

What was needed for the Church to recover its balance was a change at its centre. It was made in 1878 when a new pope, Leo XIII, was elected. A man of positive and discerning mind, he set himself the task of leading Catholic thought back to the main road of Christian tradition. One of his first acts was to create Newman a cardinal. Thereby he dissipated the cloud of official disapproval under which Newman had lived because of his liberal sympathies, in effect recommending his views to Catholics. In a series of encyclical letters, remarkable for their intelligent grasp of the modern situation and for their clear presentation of Christian guidelines for solving its problems, he set about teaching the Church: encyclicals on the Christian constitution of states (1885), on human liberty (1888), on the duties of Christians as citizens (1890), on the condition of the working class (*Rerum Novarum* 1891), and on Christian democracy (1901). In all of them he sought to recall men's minds to a sound philosophy of the state and public life.

These encyclicals did much to break down the sterile opposition of a large section of Catholic opinion to modern political developments and to encourage liberal thinking in the Catholic Church. Ideally, he said, a Christian state should have a specifically Christian constitution. But in the circumstances of the modern world it may be necessary for Christians to resign themselves to something less, and legitimate for the state to tolerate all religions 'for the sake of ensuring some great good or of avoiding some great evil' (*Immortale Dei*; DZ 3176).

Pope Leo XIII's greatest contribution to Christian social doctrine was in the field of social justice, for which he is chiefly remembered today. So important has been the development initiated by him and carried on by later popes that it merits separate treatment in a new chapter.

Chapter 5.
JUSTICE IN THE MODERN WORLD

What Samuel Coleridge said of Britain was substantially true of every country undergoing the industrial revolution in the nineteenth century: 'We have game laws, corn laws, cotton factories, Spitalfields, the tillers of the soil paid poor rates, and the remainder of the population mechanized into engines of the manufactory of the new rich men; yea, the machinery of the wealth of the nation made up of the wretchedness, disease and depravity of those who should constitute the strength of the nation.'

In 1891 Pope Leo XIII sent out an encyclical letter on the condition of the working classes which dismayed many Catholics. The pope did not stop at exhortation to the work of charitable relief, as his predecessors had done, but went on to urge major economic reforms in the name of justice and gave his blessing to working-class solidarity and state intervention. He appeared to be joining forces with Karl Marx.

In a famous passage of the *Communist Manifesto* Marx, in support of his thesis that the key to social history is the class struggle, observed that 'the bourgeoisie, wherever it got the upper hand, put an end to all feudal, patriarchal, idyllic relations, pitilessly tore asunder the motley of feudal ties that bound a man to his "natural superiors", and left remaining no other bond between man and man than naked self-interest and callous cash payment.' Pope Leo agreed about the facts, which Marx had helped to clarify; but he rejected the thesis as a whole and criticized its assumptions. In opposition to Marx's dialectical theory of class-conflict he offered a Christian project of economic cooperation.

The encyclical *Rerum Novarum* had to some extent the nature of a report. Preceded by years of investigation carried out by individuals and groups in Europe and North America, its purpose was to publish the conclusions and to prick the Christian conscience. Men like Bishop Ketteler in Germany,

Cardinal Gibbons and Archbishop Ireland in the United States of America, Cardinal Manning in Britain, and Count de Mun in France had been outspoken critics of *laissez-faire* capitalism, but owing to the conservative disposition and fears of Catholics they had won little support within the Church. Since the publication of the *Communist Manifesto* in 1848 Catholics generally had shown themselves more concerned about resisting communist influence than about changing the conditions which foster it. Many now thought it improper for the pope and bishops to intervene in the market place. Pope Leo and the men whose work and persuasion encouraged him to speak out took a different view. Its simplest expression Manning gave: 'A new task is before us. The Church has no longer to deal with Parliaments and princes, but with the masses and with the people. Whether we will or no, this is our work; we need a new spirit and a new law of life' (E. Soderini, *The Pontificate of Leo XIII*, tr. B. Carter, London 1934, vol. 1, p. 174). What surprises us today is not that Church leaders came to this conclusion but that they took so long to do so. Marx had read the signs of the times half a century earlier. He proved a false prophet, but he is to be credited with having stirred the consciences of Christians, even though unintentionally, by inspiring fear of the class war he preached.

Leo XIII plotted a course between the Scylla and Charybdis of extreme capitalism and extreme socialism. On the other hand, he condemned the *laissez-faire* doctrine that economic life should be subject only to the rule of supply and demand, insisting that like every other area of life economics should be regulated by considerations of social justice and Christian charity. On the other, he rejected as false the Marxist contention that private ownership of the means of production and profit inevitably result in the exploitation of labour by capital and the misery of the proletariat. Against this belief he held that the cause of the pitiful condition of the working classes was not the profit motive itself but its exemption from proper control. Its unregulated play resulted in the monopoly of economic power by a few magnates who were free to use it in their own selfish interest. In itself the profit motive contributes a necessary stimulus to enterprise and progress. Transference of ownership to the state would produce an even greater concentration of power and deprive the family and the individual of their proper freedom and responsibility. The function of the state is not to absorb the family and the individual but to furnish the conditions needed for their welfare, material and spiritual.

What is required, Pope Leo concluded, is a wider and fairer distribution of property, an overall supervision of its use by the state, and legal recognition of the right of workers to associate in trade unions. Organized legally, workers will be able to defend their interests and negotiate from strength with employers for fair wages, hours and conditions of work. When negotiation fails, the state has the right and duty to intervene in order to enforce the common good and remove causes of conflict between capital and labour. As for employers, their first duty is to pay those whom they employ a living wage: enough to secure a decent standard of living.

The importance of Pope Leo XIII is that he recalled Catholic thought from a *cul de sac* to the main road. In doing so he gave it a direction and impulse which initiated a fruitful development. Catholics were encouraged to abandon their attachment to the past, with its romantic idealization of the Middle Ages, and to devote their zeal to a social reconstruction based on a conception of justice traditional in principle but contemporary in application. Concern for the poor was translated into concern for the industrial proletariat; exhortation to charity into an appeal for economic justice; and negative protest into a demand for legislation designed to protect the masses of workers from exploitation and give them economic security and opportunity as their due by natural right.

Thus Leo XIII revived the tradition of constructive social criticism which began when the Church was emancipated by Constantine, reached its peak when the Church played a leading role in the society of the Middle Ages, and began to decline from the time of the Renaissance when by degrees the Church was thrust out of public affairs, until after the French Revolution the tradition was almost totally eclipsed by a growing tendency to negative protest which culminated in Pius IX's *Syllabus of Errors*.

Forty years later appeared another encylical letter on social justice, *Quadragesimo Anno* (1931). Pope Pius XI felt justified in claiming for *Rerum Novarum* that its influence had been momentous within the Catholic Church and had gone far beyond it. On the theoretical level it had given birth to 'a genuine Catholic social science'; and on the practical level it had contributed much to the improvement in the condition of the working class, especially by the encouragement it had given to the founding of trade unions and to the passing of labour laws. But he also felt it necessary to clarify some points of interpretation in dispute and to take account of changes in the situation since Pope Leo's day.

The changes which Pope Pius had in mind were to a large extent effects of the Russian Revolution. He found it necessary to revise Pope Leo's judgement on socialism and to draw a distinction, which Leo had not made, between socialism which had 'degenerated into communism' bent on class war, total abolition of private property, and eradication of religion, and socialism of a different spirit and aim. No doubt he was aware that Britism socialism, for instance, had developed under a distinctively Christian influence.

Communism Pius XI saw as the product of *laissez-faire* capitalism. Selfish individualism and ruthless competition, he argued, are self-destructive forces leading from the open market to huge impersonal monopolies, and then, as greed for wealth generates greed for power, to the absolute monopoly of state communism. So far Pius agreed with Marx. But he disagreed with Marx's belief that class war and the triumph of communism are inevitable and productive of human welfare.

Neither in *Quadragesimo Anno* nor in a later encyclical expressly on atheistic communism was Pope Pius XI's message to Catholics that their duty is to fight and hunt out communists. He urged them to work for a just social order, removing bad social conditions which induce men to seek redress in communism. Capital and labour, he wrote, need each other. Conflict between them can change into cooperation if the claims of each are regulated by the common good of the community as a whole. The proper function of the state is not to take over management of economic life but to govern it by means of just laws, leaving to private enterprise and negotiations what can be achieved by them. The principle, to which he gave the apt but ugly name of 'the principle of subsidiarity', is one of social justice, not of mere expediency.

Whereas in *Rerum Novarum* economic justice requires that workers be paid a wage sufficient for a man to support himself in health and reasonable comfort, in *Quadragesimo Anno* it demands more: a family wage such that it is unnecessary for a mother to earn, and a partnership between capital and labour. Pius XI was less opposed to public ownership than Leo XIII, allowing that in some cases the common good may require it: 'It is rightly contended that certain forms of property must be reserved to the state because they carry with them power too great to be left in private persons without harm to the community' (*QA* 114). The principle is the same for both, but with the experience of the intervening years Pius understands it better. In this sense he developed Leo's thought. At the same time he corrected as a misunderstanding the contention of some Catholics that in defending the right to private property and rejecting communism Leo had condemned nationalization and public ownership as wrong in all circumstances.

Pius XI was careful to point out that if the Church appeared to be approaching a socialist conception of social order, it was because socialism had moved nearer to the Christian position: 'It seems as if socialism were afraid of its own principles and the conclusions drawn by communists and were approaching positions which Christian tradition has always held as true. It cannot be denied that its aims sometimes come very near to the demands Christian reformers make as just' (*QA* 113).

Thirty years later the social situation came under review again. In two complementary encyclicals, *Mater et Magistra* (1961) and *Pacem in Terris* (1963), Pope John XXIII wrote about the problems of human development and the Church's role in the mass civilization of the later twentieth century. He evidently thought that enough had been done by Leo XIII, Pius XI and Pius XII to establish the broad lines of sound theory. After recapitulating their teaching, he turns to questions of practical application and of the proper Christian attitude to a world in the throes of profound social change. In so doing, however, he opens out perspectives indirectly affecting doctrine.

Mater et Magistra, written a year before the opening of the Second Vatican Council and doubtless intended as a preface, is primarily concerned with the problems of what is called 'socialization': the mounting organisation and centralized control of human life. How are the gains in health, housing, employment, education and leisure to be maintained and augmented without losses to human dignity, freedom and responsibility? To this question Pope John answers that it is possible to have the material gains of socialization without corresponding spiritual impoverishment on two conditions: if the state permits and encourages subordinate associations of people for various purposes to develop as autonomous bodies not directly subject to its control; and if these bodies permit and encourage their members to share in responsibility and to exercise personal initiative. Here the principle of subsidiarity is held to be valid, because necessary for a full human development, in every sphere of life and at every level, economic, social and political. For the same reason, we may add, it is valid in ecclesiastical life as well.

But in reaffirming Pius XI's principle that the function of the state is a subsidiary one, 'to direct, watch, stimulate and restrain', John XXIII expands the definition significantly, allowing the state a larger role, 'to direct, stimulate, coordinate, furnish and integrate' (*QA* 80; *MM* 53). While insisting that to narrow the scope for private enterprise unduly is to stifle initiative and open the way to political tyranny, he recognises that there is greater need today than before of state intervention. To prevent mass unemployment fluctuations of the economy require to be under its control.

Likewise, while affirming again the right to private

property, Pope John amends and enlarges the current conception. He draws attention to the fact that the whole conception of private property, which is generally associated today with the large possessions of the rich, has traditionally in Christian thought been linked with the small holdings of the poor, for whose dignity, freedom and responsibility it has been regarded as a suitable safeguard. Today for an increasing number of people security lies in social insurance and professional training rather than in ownership of land and goods. The notion of property has therefore to be widened and the right to it extended accordingly.

Wider perspectives affect doctrine on two other important points as well. The first concerns remuneration for work done. Justice, writes Pope John, is not always satisfied by paying adequate wages. Where there is increased productivity, all who have contributed to it are entitled to share in its profits; and when firms are successful enough to finance large development projects, the workers whom they employ have some claim on the revenues used (*MM* 75, 77). The language of the Latin text is tentative on this point, and does not specify a claim to acquire share capital. Pope John goes on to say that 'workers should gradually come to be part-owners of the company in which they work', but adds 'by whatever methods are most suitable'. The second concerns relations between employers and employed. Human dignity requires that employees should have opportunity to exercise responsibility and initiative in the affairs of the firm for which they work. With due regard for its authority and efficiency, the management should enable the workers to 'bring their experience to bear on decisions regulating their activity' and 'to have their say and make their contribution to the efficient running and development of the enterprise' (*MM* 92).

This is new but not unrelated to what previous popes had taught. A first tentative suggestion was made by Pope Pius XI: 'We consider it advisable under present conditions that as far as possible the work-contract should be modified by a partnership-contract' (*QA* 64). This suggestion was taken up and discussed by a number of Catholic social workers and writers in the years following the second world war, especially in France and Germany. Some of them began to claim a share in management for workers as a matter of natural right, arguing that it gives effect to the sense of responsibility implanted in human nature by God. The claim and the argument provoked prolonged controversy. In 1951 Pope Pius XII intervened, denying that joint management can be claimed as a right in the name of justice. Discussion, however, did not end there, and in *Mater et Magistra* Pope John XXIII also intervened, apparently conceding what Pius XII had denied: 'The exercise of responsibility by workers in factories is not only in conformity with the nature of man but is also fully in keeping with historical developments in the economic, social and political fields' (*MM* 93).

New too is the attention paid in *Mater et Magistra* to the great inequality of living standards both among different groups or classes within the same nation and between different nations. A large section is devoted to the predicament of the newly formed nations of Africa and Asia. Pope John insists that, whatever the difficulties, the rich nations are bound in conscience before God to assist the development of the poor nations generously. Besides, 'given the growing interdependence of the peoples of the earth, it is not possible to preserve peace for long if there is glaring social and economic inequality between them' (*MM* 157).

The point had been made and pressed again and again by a few alert commentators and writers after the second world war, notably among Catholics by the English economist Barbara Ward and by the French Dominicans Joseph Lebret and Yves Congar. To Pope John it seemed so important that he devoted the second encyclical, *Pacem in Terris*, wholly to the theme of the yearning of masses of men and women throughout the world for lasting peace, and the dependence of world peace on world justice. What is of special interest here is that social justice is now conceived in terms not only of equity and protection but also of personal growth. And personal growth is understood as man's development not only as an individual but also as a member of society and as a citizen.

Already in 1942 Pope Pius XII, in a broadcast message to a world at war, had given a comprehensive list of human rights as a necessary basis for a just peace. In this he anticipated, and perhaps influenced, the Universal Declaration of the Rights of Man issued in 1948 by the newly established United Nations Organisation.

The indebtedness of *Pacem in Terris* to Pope Pius XII's Christmas discourses of 1942 and 1944 is obvious and acknowledged. But, as commentators have observed, Pope John's encyclical follows more closely in approach, and sometimes even in language, the list of the UNO Declaration. Some have seen evidence here of a desire on the part of Pope John to meet the secular world in a friendly spirit on the common ground of whatever is good in its aims and endeavours. Certainly the eirenical spirit of *Pacem in Terris* inaugurated a new era in the relations of the Catholic Church to the secular world. Evidence of this is manifest in the documents of the Second Vatican Council which we will look at in the following chapter. Comparison with the *Syllabus of Errors* shows how far papal attitudes towards the modern world have changed within the past hundred years.

Recalling Pope Pius XII's teaching that the individual should not be a merely passive element in the social order, Pope John goes on to claim that in virtue of his dignity as a human person, by nature free and responsible, every man has a right to take an active part as a citizen in political affairs and contribute to the welfare and progress of the community. An indispensable condition for man's proper personal growth, and therefore an essential requirement for a just social order, is that he should have opportunity to exercise deliberation and decision in every sphere of community life, including politics. 'Human dignity requires that a man should have scope for freedom and initiative. In social relations he should exercise his rights and fulfil his obligations and in the countless forms of collaboration with other people should act chiefly on his own initiative and responsibility' (*PT* 34).

In other words, men have a right not only to be governed well but also to take part in government of the community to which they belong. Pope John adds realistically that the manner of exercising the right will depend upon the political attainment of the community. This is an important advance in Catholic political thought. Official doctrine as it now stands agrees in principle with the thought of Bellarmine, Suarez and Newman.

As far as explicit statement goes *Pacem in Terris* does not indicate preference for one form of government rather than another. Implicitly, however, it does so. To what has been summarised above it adds a plea for 'the threefold division of powers' (legislative, judicial and executive) on the grounds that it is necessary for the protection of human rights and for the prevention of the growth of totalitarianism. Since the separation of powers is a primary feature of democratic institutions, and since the active participation of all the citizens in the business of government implies a system of election and representation, it is justifiable to conclude that the encyclical indirectly indicates preference for a form of democratic government, at any rate where it is the outgrowth of historical circumstances and popular aspiration (*PT* 68,78-9).

In a fifth section on world justice and peace Pope John is emphatic that in their mutual relations nations and states are under the same moral law as individual persons and citizens to pursue the common good; only, in the case of international affairs the common good must be understood globally as the welfare and progress of 'the whole human family'. Statesmen are therefore obliged in conscience to look beyond national self-interest and strive for a working solidarity of the world community.

In this connection he urges the setting up of some form of world government. Manifestly, he says, under present conditions the common good of nations cannot be achieved by means of the conventions and treaties which sufficed in the past. The interdependence of national economies, the maldistribution of wealth among the nations, and the enormously destructive power of arms today, make it imperative to establish a world organisation with authority, power and competent agencies such as no collection of states has or can have. The required organisation can be established only by agreement. It must have as its function not to supplant national states and take over what they are competent to do, but to supply what they are unable to achieve singly or collectively. Since, however, the common good of nations, world justice and peace require world government today, they have a moral duty to cooperate in establishing it without delay. Implicit, though not stated, is that states should be willing to surrender as much of their national sovereignty as the common good demands.

In *Pacem in Terris* Pope John was concerned to stress the need and purpose of world government rather than to identify any existing organisation. Even so, he acknowledged the existence of the United Nations Organisation and praised its work as a start in the right direction. The encyclical commends the Universal Declaration of Human Rights and the aim set out in the Preamble to ensure that the 'effective recognition and observance' of these rights and freedoms should be 'a common standard of achievement for all peoples and nations'. But it expresses dissatisfaction that to date the Declaration is wholly void of legal provisions for dealing with violations of the rights it recognises (*PT* 145).

In the same connection Pope John touches on one of the thorniest problems of the contemporary world: racial antipathy and discrimination. So emotionally charged is this issue that what he has to say is best given in his own words: 'In many parts of the world there are communities made up of people of different racial origin. Their racial differences must not be made a pretext for keeping them apart and preventing them from mingling freely. It would be contrary to the realities of the contemporary world, in which distances separating peoples have been almost wiped out. And we cannot overlook the fact that, although human beings differ from one another in their racial peculiarities, they have more important attributes in common and are by nature disposed to meet one another, especially at the level of spiritual values in the assimilation of which their progress and perfection chiefly lie. All have the right and the duty to live in communion with one another' (*PT* 100).

Here *Pacem in Terris* rejects as untrue the theory that some races are by nature superior to others, and condemns as unjust the practice of racial discrimination and segregation whereby people of one race deny equal rights and freedoms to people of other races and exclude them from full participation in the life of the community. In the form in which it was preached and practised in Nazi Germany racism was condemned in 1937 by Pope Pius XI in an encyclical letter, *Mit brennender Sorge*, addressed to the German people. Pope John condemned the *apartheid* form wherever it is found and whether it is enforced by law or by custom. In this form racism became a world problem after the second world war when the old colonial empires began to be wound up and the old practices of 'the colour-bar' hardened into a more or less rigid social system and, in southern Africa, a doctrine advertised as Christian.

In neither of his encyclicals did Pope John make mention of communism or warn against the danger of it. In this he took a very different line from his predecessors, Pius XI and Pius XII. He was of course as opposed as they to the theory, but the danger evidently weighed less on his mind. In *Pacem in Terris*, drawing a distinction between erroneous doctrines and those who hold them, he recommends Catholics to collaborate with people, of other religions and none, in projects which benefit mankind. It is reasonable to think that he includes collaboration with Communists (*PT* 158).

Equally unprecedented in papal statements are Pope John's words on religious toleration: 'We must also include among human rights the right to be free to worship God according to the dictates of a right conscience and to practise religion in public as well as in private' (*PT* 14). No section of *Pacem in Terris* gave rise after its publication to more discussion among Catholics.

Can it be that a person has a real right to profess in public as well as in private a religion which is in reality false but which he believes to be true? The common answer of Catholics to this question has been that in such cases there can be no real or objective right but only a supposed or subjective right. This has sometimes been expressed in the brief but misleading phrase 'error has no rights'. The meaning of the formula as correctly used is that, since it can never be morally right to profess and practise what is false, there can be no moral right to profess and practise a false religion. To those who do not accept the Catholic religion as the true religion, or the only true religion, the argument may appear to amount to nothing better than a defence of religious intolerance, and Pope John's recognition of the principle of religious toleration will be seen by them as a welcome departure from a regrettable Catholic tradition.

But these are theoretical considerations with which Pope John was not concerned. His encyclical leaves us in no doubt that the right of every person to freedom of worship must be recognised and upheld in practice. In effect he cut the argument short and gave to the principle of religious toleration more explicit and unambiguous acknowledgement than any pope had done before. The point was taken up and emphatically endorsed by the Second Vatican Council, to which we now turn.

Chapter 6.
THE SECOND VATICAN COUNCIL

When Pope John XXIII announced his intention of calling a general council of the Church, the need of it was far from obvious to most Catholics. In two thousand years of Christian history there had been only twenty general councils and every one of them had been convoked to deal with some great crisis in the Church: heresy, schism, or scandal. In 1959 there appeared to be no comparable cause for anxiety. Catholic faith and practice seemed sound enough. Unity was not threatened. In most areas of the world the Catholic Church was tolerated and generally respected. All seemed well. Pope John thought otherwise. To him it was plain that the Church, charged by Christ to bring good news to mankind, was not carrying out its mission effectively in the twentieth century.

From the time of Pope Leo XIII, as we have seen, the Catholic Church had adopted an increasingly positive attitude to the modern world. Yet in the middle of the century it was living alongside the world it exists to transform, still too withdrawn to act as leaven in contemporary society. This defect Pope John set himself to correct. He brought to the task two great qualities of his own. He had an eye for what is true and good in the trends of society today, and he set out to meet the world with an eagerness and joy suited to a bearer of good news. He openly dissociated himself from 'the prophets of woe' who can see only disaster in the direction in which the world is moving; and in the current tendency to call in question the assumptions, practices and structures of the past he saw more than an evil spirit of restlessness and irresponsibility, discerning rather the hand of Providence 'leading us towards a new order of human relations in fulfilment of the divine purpose in human history' (Pope John's opening address, *The Documents of Vatican II*, ed. W. Abbott, pp. 712-3).

The Second Vatican Council which met in the years 1962-65 had a better title to be called 'ecumenical' than any previous general council of the Church. Never before had so many bishops assembled in conference; never before had they been men of every race, colour, culture, language and region; never before had a council of the Roman Catholic Church been attended by observers of all, or nearly all, the main Christian communions. These facts alone would have ensured that Vatican II had a wider outlook than Vatican I; but that its horizon was worldwide was due to the desire and determination of the majority of the bishops.

The openness of Vatican II to the contemporary world is stamped on all its documents and most markedly on the *Constitution on the Church in the Modern World* and on the *Declaration on Religious Freedom* which concern us in this chapter. These, the most strenuously debated decrees of the Council, were promulgated only on its last working day. It was appropriate that the bishops ended on a note of concern for people who are not Catholics but their brothers throughout the world.

Not since New Testament times has the Catholic Church been so outward-looking as the Second Vatican Council made it. The change taking place does not, however, please everybody. Some Catholics welcome it as a sign of growing maturity in the spirit of Christ, but others are deeply disturbed and see in it a decline into the spirit of the world, or at least a dangerous opening to its influence. Opinion was similarly divided in New Testament times once the Church began to move outwards from Palestine. There was rejoicing on the part of some Christians and dismay on the part of others when the church not only admitted large numbers of Greeks to baptism but also set about adapting itself to the Hellenistic world. Paul, Barnabas and Peter were opposed as innovators. But when the first council of the Church was convened at Jerusalem, the decision was in favour of adaptation and liberty in all but essentials (Acts 11;15). Not only did the Church survive, but it grew in understanding of the universalism and freedom of the Gospel.

What the Council of Jerusalem did for the Church in the first century the Second Vatican Council tried to do for it in the twentieth, as is evident in its conclusions. We shall have to confine our attention to a few major points of development concerned with the Christian 'presence and activity in the world' (*CCMW* 2): that is, the proper relation of the Church to the contemporary world in general and to the state in particular.

The distinctive note sounded by the *Constitution on the Church in the Modern World* is that the Church is in the world to serve the world as did Jesus Christ who 'entered the world to give witness to the truth, to rescue and not to sit in judgement' (*CCMW* 3). This declaration of purpose is important. It bears a warning to Catholics and an assurance to other people who, rightly or wrongly, have judged the Catholic Church as willing to work with the world only for its own advantage, to take but not to give. Accordingly, addressing themselves 'not only to the Church and all who invoke the name of Christ, but also to the whole of humanity', the bishops offered the disinterested services of the Catholic Church in the work of championing the dignity and freedom of the human person and of fostering the brotherhood of men (*CCMW* 40-43).

What the bishops committed the Church to appears especially in their declarations that the equality of men must receive increasing recognition in the social order, and that all forms of discrimination contrary to it must be eradicated (*CCMW* 29,42,27). The reasons given, one old, the other new, enunciate two fundamental principles which must govern the social order if it is to be truly human. Whatever their differences of birth, talent and attainment, all men are basically equal by virtue of their natural dignity and supernatural destiny; whatever in social institutions and practices insults human dignity by treating men as tools rather than as responsible persons is pernicious to society as poison is to the body. It destroys life.

Among examples of pernicious institutions and practices given in the *Constitution* is slavery, and the fact that it is listed alongside of prostitution leaves us in no doubt that slavery is condemned in principle. Thus in effect Augustine's theoretical justification of slavery as a penalty for sin is dismissed as erroneous, and the curious tradition whereby it was perpetuated for so many centuries in the pages of Catholic textbooks is brought at long last to an end.

Documentary evidence of the persistence of this tradition in Catholic thought is amply furnished in a recent study to which we are indebted here, (*The Development of Catholic Social Doctrine concerning Slavery*, by J.F. Maxwell, *World Justice Quarterly*, vol. 11, nn. 2 and 3, 1969-70). The author shows that the Augustinian view, although not universally accepted, influenced popes, theologians and Church councils for close on 1,500 years. Space permits only a few illustrations.

Pope Gregory I (590-604), known to history as Gregory the Great because of his reforming zeal and saintly character, evidently did not think slavery wrong in principle. In many of his letters he referred to the practice of his day, not to condemn it but to give advice to his clients, clerical and lay, about owning, buying and selling slaves. To some he recommended manumission, but as an act of charity, not as a duty in justice. It is of him that the story is told that seeing sturdy flaxen-haired Britons on sale in the Roman market he exclaimed: 'They are not Angles but angels!' Admiration inspired him with desire, not apparently to liberate them, but to convert their compatriots. So he sent a band of missionaries to Britain headed by the Augustine who founded the see of Canterbury.

The collection of ecclesiastical laws compiled by Gratian at a later date (about 1140) includes a number of earlier canons on slavery which show that Gregory's mind and the canon law of the time agreed. Augustinian theory then appeared to fit social fact. For the barbarians who invaded western Europe from the fifth century brought in and installed their own customary practice of slavery, sweeping away the social progress made in the preceding centuries and putting the clock back for a long time to come. The Church did not oppose the new slavery but sought to alleviate its harshness, upholding the rights of marriage for Christian slaves as far as lay in its power.

In subsequent centuries when slaves gradually developed

into serfs and then, in the more prosperous areas of Europe, became free men, there were cases of local Church councils objecting to the evils of slavery in their own regions; but the traditional view of its theoretical morality remained unchanged. Reappraisal and growth of a liberal view were impeded by the interests and conflicts of the age: the study of Roman law and the application of its principles to medieval society; the rediscovery of Aristotle with his doctrine that some men are by nature fit only to be slaves; the Saracen siege of Europe and enslavement of Christian captives; the lucrative trade of coastal towns with Saracen galleys in slaves, arms and equipment; and the notion of a *ius gentium* (international customary law) as authorising the penalty of slavery for collective as well as for individual crimes.

Centuries of armed struggle with the Saracens and the resultant isolation of Europe from the outside world bred in Christian society the firm conviction that non-European peoples were one and all, like the Saracens, fiercely warlike enemies of Christ who had to be conquered by arms before they could be converted to the Gospel. And so from the eleventh to the fifteenth century popes commissioned Christian warriors to march in Crusades against the Saracens and wrest the Holy Land from their control; and in the fifteenth and sixteenth centuries popes authorised Christian kings to invade and occupy the newly discovered territories of West Africa and the Americas enslaving the inhabitants as a penalty for resistance and a means to their conversion.

Typical of the latter period and its popes was Nicholas V who in 1452 addressed a Brief to King Alfonso V of Portugal granting him and his son, Henry the Navigator, permission to annex Lagos and subject its population of 'Saracens, pagans, and other enemies of Christ' to perpetual slavery.

An exception was made for baptized Christians and catechumens. From the fifteenth to the nineteenth century a number of papal decrees forbade their enslavement under penalty of excommunication. These decrees were occasioned by letters sent by missionaries in the Atlantic islands and the Americas to popes and kings in Europe, appealing to them to intervene against the pitiless enslavement of the natives by the Portuguese and Spanish conquerors. In some cases the prohibition was extended in favour of all the native people.

In the same period, however, slavery was at times sanctioned by popes to meet practical needs concerned with public welfare, such as the administration of the city of Rome and the manning of the papal fleet. Hence it is clear that the papal decrees condemned the practice of slavery in the new world, not slavery itself. No change was made in the canon law of the Church, which continued to permit it.

The awakening of conscience to the evil of slavery and the movement for its abolition were instigated outside the Catholic Church among French revolutionaries and American and British Protestants. Catholics were influenced, but slowly. Pope Pius VII gave support at the Congress of Vienna (1815) to efforts aimed at putting a stop to the international trade in African slaves, but his successors in the papal office did not follow up his initiative. And Catholic theologians generally found difficulty in changing their minds about the morality of slavery because its theological justification was so traditional in the Church as to appear to belong to the Catholic faith itself. Not surprisingly, Catholics in North America were given little or no encouragement by their clergy to support the abolitionist movement, and Catholic slave-owners were not disturbed in conscience.

The break with the old tradition began with Pope Leo XIII. He encouraged Cardinal Lavigerie, founder of the White Fathers, in his anti-slavery campaign; he wrote against the evils of slavery to the bishops of Brazil in the year of its emancipation of slaves (1881); above all, in his encyclical letter *Rerum Novarum* (1891) he undermined the old theory by denying the validity of the distinction between dominion over the persons and dominion over the labour of slaves, a distinction which theologians had commonly made in defence of slave-ownership. But only when the Second Vatican Council explicitly condemned slavery as immoral in principle was the break complete and the old tradition of doctrine finally discredited.

The Catholic Church has not gone on record as the protagonist of the economic, social and political rights of man in the eighteenth and nineteenth centuries when the struggle was at its height. A number of laymen and a few of the clergy took up the cause; but the popes and the main body of bishops remained aloof or lent their influence to the *ancien regime*. The victories won owed little to the Catholic Church before Pope Leo XIII. It is therefore disappointing and out of tune with the general frankness and modesty of the Vatican Council that, without confessing this shortcoming, the *Constitution* roundly asserts that 'by virtue of the Gospel committed to her, the Church proclaims the rights of man, and acknowledges and holds in high esteem the dynamic movements of today by which these rights are everywhere fostered' (*CCMW* 41).

However, the *Constitution* is directly concerned with the present and the future, and it gives warm recognition to the work of others in the past. What is new in its message is the emphasis it lays on human dignity. This is now the central concern of Catholic social doctrine summed up in the memorable formula that the Church 'is at once the sign and safeguard of the transcendence of the human person' (*CCMW* 76).

In this formula the Council set the direction for Catholic social thought and action. Observing that society is not static but always on the move, and never more so than in the present age, it declared that 'before it lies the path to freedom or to slavery, to progress or to retreat, to brotherhood or to hatred' (*CCMW* 9). It therefore called for a better ordering of society on the basis of human dignity and freedom, and for a corresponding change of heart and purpose in men.

Foremost among the changes needed is the elimination of every form of discrimination, 'whether cultural or social, whether based on sex, race, colour, social condition, language or religion', which infringes fundamental human rights and offends against human dignity. Another is the extension of the conception of a just social order to take in the whole world: 'The common good, that is, the sum of those social conditions which enable groups and their members to progress in mounting freedom to their full development, takes on an increasingly universal character involving the rights and duties of the whole human race. It is the duty of every group to take account of the needs and legitimate aspirations of other groups and indeed of the whole human family' (*CCMW* 26,29,31).

Thus like Pope John XXIII the Second Vatican Council implicitly condemned all forms and degrees of racial discrimination and *apartheid.* Itself in composition a microcosm of the contemporary world, it was well aware of the difficulty to which differences of race and colour give rise. But it did not allow that it can ever be morally tolerable to make such differences the principle of social order or that historical conditioning can be accepted as a valid excuse for acquiescence and neglect to take steps to change such a social order where it is established. It described social order of the kind as 'disgraceful' because it is offensive to human dignity and therefore 'dishonours the Creator in the highest degree' (*CCMW* 27,28).

Some of the bishops wanted *apartheid* to be condemned by name. Most, however, saw it as a form of discrimination included in the general condemnation, and preferred to centre the condemnation on an error of principle rather than on a particular manifestation of it. Beyond question *apartheid* stands condemned in principle by the Council on the theological ground that it is contrary to God's intention since 'God, who has a fatherly care for everyone, has willed that men should constitute one family and treat one another in a spirit of brotherhood' (*CCMW* 24).

In regard to Church-state relations the Council's teaching is traditional, yet new. It goes back to the ideas which, as we have noted, were developed by Bellarmine and Suarez but which had been lost to view in the dust of controversy during the years of revolutionary struggle in Church and state; and it gives them a new force by withdrawing the Church's old claim to a position of privilege in society. Now the Catholic Church 'does not put her trust in privileges conferred by civil authority. What is more, she is ready to renounce the exercise of legitimately acquired rights when it becomes clear that their use puts the disinterested character of her witness into doubt or when new conditions of life demand new arrangements' (*CCMW* 76).

What new arrangements fit the present age are indicated in the *Declaration on Religious Freedom*. The key phrase is that 'in what concerns the Church's relations to governments and the whole social order the fundamental principle is its freedom to preach the Gospel to every creature' (*DRF* 13). This freedom is explained as immunity from external interference and control, immunity necessary for the Church to do its proper work of worship and witness. It is claimed as a right. But it is a negative claim on civil government not to hinder the Church from carrying out its evangelical mission, not a positive claim on the state to assist the Church in its work by defending and promoting religious truth as such.

Newman would have been well satisfied. A century earlier he wrote: 'Catholics must judge governments, not by their subservience to the temporal interests of the Church, but by the test whether they guarantee and promote the authority of conscience.' And against Manning: 'What the pope wants is, not a positive right of governing, but a negative right of not being governed; not a centre of political power, but a basis of independence' (Cf. J. Altholz, *The Liberal Catholic Movement in England*, London 1962, pp. 56, 176).

To freedom in this sense, the *Declaration* explains, the Church has a twofold title. First, it is founded on Christ's mandate to preach the Gospel publicly and to live by it. This is a theological title which the state cannot be expected to accept because it is incompetent to judge its validity. Second, it is founded on a truth about human nature: the dignity of the human person and his need of freedom to live his life, especially his religious life, fittingly in society. This is a secular title of human right which the state, as the guardian of the secular order, is by nature committed to defend. It is this second title which the Church presents today.

The distinction of titles to religious freedom is of great ecumenical importance. It makes clear that the different Churches and religious bodies all have an equal right to free-

dom which is solidly based on the same foundation of the
dignity of the human person and his need of freedom. The
Council could not have been more explicit. Religious freedom
is declared to be a matter of fundamental right, not of mere
expediency. It must be written into political constitutions and
be upheld by law. Even in countries where, for historical
reasons, special legal recognition is given in the constitution to
one religious body or Church, the right of all to equal freedom
must be conceded and made effective in practice without
discrimination. For the equality of all the citizens before the
law is 'integral to the common good of society'. But precisely
because the title on which religious freedom is claimed for all
Churches belongs to the socio-political order, it does not imply
equality of truth in their respective theologies. The *Declaration* does not blur doctrinal differences but declares their
resolution to be a matter for theological dialogue and not for
political pressure (*DRF* 2,3).

From defining the proper relation between Church and
state in terms of religious freedom the Council went on to
draw conclusions concerning the political order which are
unprecedented in official formulations of Catholic doctrine.
Church and state have each its own distinct sphere of responsibility in which it is autonomous; but as both exist to serve the
welfare of the same members of society, though by different
titles, neither is wholly independent of the other. They can
fulfil their proper functions only by collaboration, not by
mere coexistence; for besides its own distinct sphere of
activity, each has a service to render in the sphere of the other.
For the state it is to give favourable recognition to the
Church's proper activity; and for the Church it is to concern
itself with the moral and religious values involved in public
affairs (*DRF* 6; *CCMW* 76).

In this context occurs one of the very few condemnations
uttered by the Council: 'Disapproval must be expressed for
those forms of government found in some countries which
fetter civil and religious liberty'; for 'it is inhuman for political
authority to assume totalitarian and dictatorial forms which
violate personal and group rights' (*CCMW* 73,75).

The connection made by the Council between religious and other freedoms, and the condemnation of illiberal forms of government, constitute a major advance in Catholic social thought of great practical as well as theoretical importance. As though to wipe away traces of past suspicion of political liberalism, the bishops pronounced a remarkable eulogy of freedom in the *Constitution* and the *Declaration*. Freedom is said to be 'the preeminent sign of the divine nature in man'. The value put upon it by 'our contemporaries' is to be applauded. The mounting demand made in the world today for constitutional change, civil liberty, free institutions, open opportunity and universal franchise is evidence not of growing irresponsibility in modern man but of his 'keener awareness of human dignity'. In spite of adverse social conditions still to be overcome the bishops felt confident that 'modern man is on the road to a fuller development of his personality and an increasing discovery and vindication of his rights'. Accordingly, they had a special word of praise for 'those national procedures which allow the greatest number of citizens to take part in public affairs with real freedom'. In political life traditions merit respect as guides only if they in turn respect human rights (*CCMW* 17, 31, 35, 41, 73, 75; *DRF* 1).

Here as elsewhere the Council, without tying the Church to any particular political system, expressed clear preference for democratic forms of government. In doing so it laid the Catholic Church open to the charge of belying its avowed principles in its own practice. For theological reasons which cannot be gone into here, the Church is not governed democratically in its decisions concerning matters of faith and morals. The procedures of the Council itself, while permitting a freedom of debate which surprised non-Catholic observers, were not strictly democratic. It is not, however, inconsistent for those who accept the theology, and believe that religious truth is attained otherwise, to hold that in other spheres of life human welfare is best served by democratic processes. That is not to say that there is no place within the Catholic Church for democratic procedures outside the area of doctrine, such as in the appointment of officers, the conduct of administration, and the extension of lay responsibility. Indeed, the Vatican Council set the Catholic Church on a course of greater freedom of discussion, more open theology, and closer consultation which, despite resistance in some quarters, have become features of its life since.

That the Church is indebted to social developments in the secular world and has much to learn from them the bishops at the Council frankly acknowledged. Such humility in regard to the achievements of the secular world is new in Catholic ecclesiastical documents. More sharply than anything else it marks the Council's intention of opening a new epoch in the history of the Church's relations with the world.

Coupled with it is a humble confession of Catholic failures to give expression to religious faith in social and political service. This neglect on the part of many Catholics the *Constitution* sees as due to a mistaken belief that religion has nothing to do with economics and politics (*CCMW* 43). Among the shortcomings which the bishops had in mind was perhaps the failure of Catholics to appreciate and support liberal movements in the past century and a half. At any rate they called upon Catholics to join other people of good will in contemporary efforts to produce a new world order of justice, peace and unity among nations, leading to some form of world government (*CCMW* 33, 42, 84, 88). In this they followed the lead given by Pope John XXIII in his encyclical *Pacem in Terris* (1963), and by Pope Paul VI in his address to the United Nations Organisation (1964). The bishops appealed for immediate support for international agencies working to relieve hunger and poverty in destitute regions of the world, to provide them with food, health services and education, and to stimulate their economic growth and help them cope with the problem of rapid increase of population resulting from births, migration and refugees (*CCMW* 84). They praised what has already been achieved. Although UNO and its agencies are not mentioned in the *Constitution* by name, reference to them is unmistakable.

Anxiety about the birth-rate and its threat to resource supply has become widespread only within recent decades.

The basic statistics have been much publicised and are now widely known. At its present growth rates the population of the world is doubling every 35 years. They are highest in the poorer countries with least resources and a constant threat of famine. Whether population growth is a cause or a symptom of contemporary social problems is open to question, but that the problems are real and grave is not.

The Vatican Council considered the issues of population-growth and birth-limitation, but its pronouncement on them disappointed the hopes of many, not so much in what it said as by what it left unsaid. The bishops noted the problems and anxieties for the world community in general and for the poor nations in particular which the high birthrate of the present time is causing. In their conclusion they did not play down the gravity of the situation or advocate blind trust in Providence, as Catholics have tended to do. They acknowledged the urgent need of family-planning as well as of economic and technical development. At the same time they insisted on the right and duty of parents: that it is the right of parents and not of the state to make a responsible decision about the size of their family, having regard to their means and circumstances, the proper care and education of their children, and the welfare of society; and that it is their duty to limit the number of their children only by means approved by the Church as morally acceptable.

The use of mechanical devices had been forbidden by Pope Pius XI. The use of the 'safe period' had been permitted by Pope Pius XII. Subsequently another and more effective method of birth control had been found and made available in the form of contraceptive pills. Many Catholics hoped that the Council would investigate the whole question of birth-control anew and, taking into account on the one hand the urgent need to limit population-growth and on the other the different nature of 'the pill', would find in favour of the morality of the new method. They argued that the use of contraceptive pills to regulate births does not differ in principle from the use of the safe period, and that it is not, like mechanical devices, a method of direct birth prevention.

The Council discussed marriage and the family at length but skirted the question of birth-control in the *Constitution on the Modern World*. It did so for no other reason then that this issue was excluded from its agenda. At the beginning of the Second Vatican Council in 1962 Pope John XXIII appointed a small commission of priests and laymen to study the question. After his death his successor, Pope Paul VI, enlarged the commission in 1964 but, alarmed by its interim report, reserved the issue to himself for decision and discouraged discussion of it in the Council (Cf. *The Agonizing Choice: Birth Control, Religion and the Law*, by N. St John-Stevas, London 1971, pp. 106-7).

In 1968, more than two years after the close of the Vatican Council, Pope Paul gave judgement in his encyclical *Humanae Vitae*. Rejecting the majority in favour of a minority report, he declared all methods of regulating birth to be illicit which involve an action 'which, either in anticipation of the conjugal act or in its accomplishment or in the development of its natural consequences proposes, whether as an end or as a means, to render procreation impossible'. The only exception he allowed is their therapeutic use as a means of curing organic diseases, and then only if it is necessary and if the foreseen result of preventing procreation is not directly intended (*HV* 14,15). Thus by implicaton, though not by name, he excluded the method of contraceptive pills as a morally acceptable method of birth control.

Pope Paul was deeply concerned about population trends, the plight of the poor nations, and the difficulty of Catholics in family planning, as his encyclicals *Populorum Progressio* and *Humanae Vitae* attest. But he was no less concerned to uphold the teaching about marriage which all the main Christian churches taught until the present century and which both the Catholic and the Orthodox churches retain: the doctrine that it is contrary to God's will, because contrary to nature, for husband and wife deliberately to exclude procreation from the marriage act. He fully recognized the gravity of the problem of the birth-rate for married couples and for society, and he shared the mounting anxiety of people today to find an effective method of limiting it. But he was unable to agree that the new method of 'the pill' differs essentially from the older methods of birth prevention condemned by the Church. Accordingly, while by implication condemning the new method, he urged the medical profession to press on in search of a method of birth-control acceptable to the Christian conscience.

He was well aware that many Catholics would find his ruling hard to accept and put into practice, and that they would suffer acute distress of conscience in consequence. He therefore asked national hierarchies to commend and explain the ruling to their people. The statements of those conferences which numbered among their members bishops of theological distinction who contributed most to the discussions of the Second Vatican Council merit special attention. While others did little more than paraphrase and summarize *Humanae Vitae*, they interpreted its practical meaning to the Church. One of the clearest and most helpful explanations came from the French bishops who summed up thus: 'Contraception can never be a good thing. It is always a disorder, but this disorder is not always sinful. It can happen that married couples consider themselves faced with a genuine conflict of duties. . . . On this subject we simply recall the constant moral teaching: when one faces a choice of duties in which one cannot avoid an evil whatever the decision may be, traditional wisdom requires that one seek before God to find which is the greater duty under the circumstances. The married couple will decide for themselves after reflecting together with all the care that the grandeur of their conjugal vocation requires' (*The Tablet*, 16 November 1968; cf. St John-Stevas, *op. cit.*, p. 198 n.2. The words 'under the circumstances', omitted in translation from the French, have been restored).

In their statement the hierarchy of England and Wales kept close to the text of *Humanae Vitae* but added the important gloss: 'It must be stated that the primacy of conscience is not in dispute. The pope, bishops, clergy and faithful must all be true to conscience. But we are bound to do everything in our power to make sure that our conscience is truly informed.

Neither the encyclical nor any other document of the Church takes away from us our right and duty to follow our conscience' (*The Tablet*, 28 September 1968; cf. St John-Stevas, *op. cit.*, p. 157).

In regard to the limitation of births critics have pointed out that *Humanae Vitae* offers least help to those who need it most. In large areas of the world struggling to overcome sub-human living conditions and the constant threat of famine, millions of indigent people are too unsophisticated to regulate births by the method of the safe period with the accurate calculations it requires. Contraceptive pills being forbidden, Catholics among them are left only the method of extended periods of total abstinence from intercourse. As the great Protestant theologian Karl Barth observed, such abstinence would be heroic to a degree beyond the capacity of most people; and perhaps, as other critics contend, it would be psychologically disturbing and injurious to the marriage. It is of interest to note that periodic abstinence was what Mahatma Gandhi, founder and hero of modern India, recommended to his people as the only method of birth control tolerable to *Brahmacharya* (the Hindu principle of self-restraint in pursuit of purity of life) because alone conducive to spiritual and bodily health and vigour (*Selected Writings of Mahatma Gandhi*, ed. R. Duncan, London 1971, ch. 6).

Humanae Vitae did not end questioning among Catholics as intended; it immediately became a major subject of controversy itself. Within the ranks not only of the laity but also of the clergy, its validity and authority were at first openly contested. Then, as pressure was put on the clergy, those unable to accept the encyclical's ruling were induced not to speak against it in public. Even at the synods of representative bishops, held periodically in Rome since the Second Vatican Council, the problems of population-growth and birth-control have not come up for further discussion.

But the debate goes on in private. Catholics are divided. Some maintain that the main issue is now one of fundamental loyalty to the pope and the Church; others that it remains concerned with the soundness of *Humanae Vitae* itself. The encyclical modifies the traditional view of marriage. Procreation is no longer held to be its primary and mutual love its secondary end. Marriage is seen as a totality in which both ends are of equal importance. But it does not allow that mutual love may be pursued to the deliberate exclusion of procreation in any act of intercourse. Criticism centres on this point.

Chapter 7.
CHANGE AND CONTINUITY

We set out to answer the question whether or in what sense the social doctrine of the Catholic Church today is the same as the teaching of Jesus Christ recorded in the New Testament writings. We have noted what popes, bishops, councils and theologians have thought age by age. What has emerged is that there have been many changes in thought and practice and that these have been related to changes in secular society. No less clearly, Christians have at all times taken the Gospel to be good news for society as much as for individual men and women. Although conditioned by their social environment, the best of them have judged it by the standard of the Gospel as they understood it, and have endeavoured to inspire society with a spirit of brotherhood and to relieve the distress of its unfortunate members.

Evident too is a tension in the life of the Church between social passivity and social activity. On the one hand there has been a tendency to acquiesce in the established order of society as being the affair of 'the world' with which the Church is not concerned; on the other a tendency to be solicitous about the character of 'society', for the salvation of which the Church is responsible to Christ. In so far as either has been dominant at any time and place, the Church has been conservative or progressive. But the tension between these two tendencies has prevented the Church as a whole from ever being wholly indifferent to or wholly engrossed in social reform. It has engendered a slow and fluctuating but continuous movement in social attitude and doctrine.

It remains for us to examine what kind of movement has been going on. A movement of continuity in change, some sort of evolution of doctrine, or a movement of contradiction and substitution? It will suffice for us to consider the kind of change made from time to time in Christian thought concerning two fundamental issues which illustrate the whole process:

property and freedom. Some repetition is unavoidable, but it will be kept as brief as possible.

* * * * *

In regard to property Jesus sought to inculcate a true sense of values. He was poor himself, and during his public career he lived on a common purse. But he did not disdain material possessions or condemn private ownership. Rather, he saw in them both a valuable means of moral growth and a serious danger. They afford men opportunity to practise generosity to other men, but they tend to captivate men's hearts and distract them from the main business of life, the service of God and neighbour in which both personal and social excellence consist. As Jesus put it, material treasure should be converted into spiritual treasure in the kingdom of God (Mt 6.21; 13.44; 19.21; Mk 10.21; Lk 12.21, 34; 18.22).

After Jesus' departure his disciples, following his example, formed a close-knit community in which property was held in common. They did not repudiate secular society, but their way of life constituted an implied criticism of the social order and its values. Common ownership, however, ceased in Jerusalem when the city fell to the Romans under Titus, and was not reproduced elsewhere. So a change was made, a change not of principle but of understanding and application. For experience led Christians to see that community of property was but an expression of that community of love which is the basic social principle of the Gospel.

At a later date, it is true, the initial communism was revived in communities of monks, and it has continued to this day in religious orders of men and women. To that extent it has been upheld as an ideal. The Church did not, however, endorse the opinion of many early theologians that private ownership is a consequence of sin and tolerable only as a practical expedient. The view which came to be traditional doctrine was that private property is natural and necessary for the common good of society, and precisely for that reason always subject to social obligations.

108

The face of Europe was changed by the barbarian invasions, and the Church took on many of the features of the feudal order which they introduced. In return for its assistance in establishing law and order, the Gothic kings endowed the Church liberally with land. By the Middle Ages the Church was one of the great landlords. From this position it gained security and independence from secular control, but at the price of involvement in secular affairs. For long ages it was a pillar of the established social and political order, party at times to its reforms but opposed to its reconstruction.

Wealth, power, social eminence and political involvement led to scandals in the life of the Church, but not to corruption of doctrine or to neglect of the poor. The doctrine that the earth's resources are God's gifts to all men was not trimmed to suit the interests of the rich. It was interpreted, in keeping with the circumstances and needs of the age, as demanding security of land-tenure based on feudal contract, prohibition of usury as exploitation of misfortune, provision of just wages and prices, and prevention of monopoly in the necessities of life. The chief beneficiaries were the poor. The mass of the people looked to the Church for protection and found it under the Church's patronage. Within the established order the Church stood for justice and used its wealth and power to supply social services which today are provided by the state: social relief; medical care; education and training; law and administration; supervision of the economy. In short, as Kenneth Clark has indicated in his television series, the Church was for many centuries the chief agent of civilization in Europe, the chief patron of the arts and crafts, and the sole guardian of moral values.

The demands referred to above were seen to be demands not of mere expediency but of equity. As such they belonged to the moral order which it was the office of the Church to elucidate. A whole moral theology of economic life was elaborated on the basis of the evangelical precepts and the philosophical notion of 'the natural law', an ideal standard of justice which it was in everybody's interest to live by and by which the equity of economic arrangements and practices was to be judged.

No comparable development of social doctrine was made until the last decade of the nineteenth century. By then it was long overdue. In the intervening centuries had occurred a profound economic revolution which ushered in the age of modern capitalism and a schism which split Europe and the Church in two. Dislodged from its traditional position at the centre of society and preoccupied with a struggle to stem the tide of religious revolt, the Catholic Church became increasingly conservative and negatively critical of the new age dawning. It had no objection in principle to capitalism. As hitherto, it criticized only the tendency of capitalists to make the acquisition of wealth the main purpose of life. As long as capitalists were religious men who acknowledged the subordination of economic to moral values, such criticism was relevant and sufficient. But by the nineteenth century capitalism had undergone a profound change and something more radical was required.

By then the notion had gained currency that economic life is subject to no law except the so-called law of supply and demand. In consequence the masses of the toiling poor were plunged in the miseries of ruthless exploitation. Partly in reaction to this situation, Marx and Engels in the *Communist Manifesto* expounded the contrary notion that the whole capitalist system should actively and would inevitably be swept away by a revolt of the masses and be replaced by a communist order of society directed and controlled by the state as sole owner until the state itself would no longer be needed. The Catholic Church had no objection in principle to communism of the kind initially practised by Christians; but it was, and always will be, irreconcilably opposed to Marxist communism with its dedication to atheism, total abolition of private ownership, complete subjection of the person to the state, and promotion of class war in pursuit of its goals.

From the close of the nineteenth century until the present time Catholic social thought has undergone a development which stage by stage has reflected the growing complexity of the economic conditions to which it has been addressed.

Pope Leo XIII assessed the situation of his day correctly. It may be that he saw class conflict narrowly as a programme rather than as a potent historical factor of social change, and so missed much of Marx's point. Yet he discerned the cause of conflict accurately. The evils of nineteenth-century capitalism were rooted in the individualism of unregulated private enterprise, the effects of which had been to concentrate economic power in the hands of a few rich capitalists and to subject the mass of wage-earners to virtual slavery.

The remedy, Pope Leo held, was not to be found in state communism, which would only aggravate the disorder, but in a wide distribution of property in the form of fair wages and working conditions. For this to be achieved the state would have to supervise the economy. The aim should not be to eliminate private property but to control its use in the interests of the whole community. Thus Pope Leo upheld the traditional guiding principle of Christian social doctrine but gave it a new application suited to the conditions of industrialized society. He enlarged the concept of property to include just wages and conditions as the first charge on profits.

Pope Pius XI went further. Having in mind the massive build-up of industry since Leo's day and the increasing concentration of economic power which it necessitated, Pius XI sanctioned not only the state's supervising the economy but also its taking over management and even ownership. But he did so only for cases of huge enterprises which put such power into private hands as operate incorrigibly against the common good.

By the mid-twentieth century the situation had changed again. Rapid growth of populations and increasing interdependence of people and nations demanded coordination of economic activity and planning of welfare and development on an unprecedented scale. Accordingly, Pope John XXIII and the Second Vatican Council advocated a far higher degree of state direction and control. At the same time they asserted the right of wage-earners to share in the management and profits of industry. Furthermore they urged as a moral duty binding on individuals and nations that a concerted effort be made to bring about a more equitable distribution of wealth within each nation and between nations in the interests of world justice and peace. Supplementing this doctrine, Pope Paul VI stressed the duty of the rich nations to assist the development of the poor nations of the world. For the welfare of the poor the whole human family is responsible to God who has bestowed the resources of the earth for the benefit of all its members.

At the time when these pronouncements were made some commentators remarked that the Catholic Church had turned about from opposition to advocacy of socialism. Certainly, the Catholic Church has changed in attitude to state control. It now advocates rather more than less of it, but only because in contemporary circumstances a large measure of state direction and control is a necessary means to a wide and fair sharing out of property in the form of wages, profits, pensions, social insurance and active participation in the management of industry by all who give their services to it. Yet what recent popes and the Vatican Council have laid down as official doctrine does not differ essentially from what Pope Gregory the Great taught in the sixth century: 'The earth is common to all, and brings forth nurture for all alike. When we furnish the destitute with any necessity we render them what is theirs, we do not bestow on them what is ours: we pay the debt of justice rather than perform the works of charity' (Cf. W. Shewring, *Rich and Poor in Christian Tradition. Writings of Many Centuries*, London 1948, p. 70).

With regard to freedom, Jesus set an example in his personal relations which many Christians have been slow to follow. He cut across the established social divisions and conventions and at the root of pride and prejudice underlying them. Generally speaking, Christians have assimilated the social outlook of their time and place.

Initially it was not so. In the evangelical spirit of brotherhood no distinctions between Jew and Gentile, free and slave, male and female, high and low, rich and poor, were observed in the first Christian communities, as the New Testament records testify.

During its first three centuries the Church did not, however, attempt to carry its ideas of human equality and freedom beyond its own fellowship. Being an unlawful body and still comparatively small, it accepted passively the established order of society, founded though it was on distinctions of wealth and power. It concerned itself only with its own freedom to worship the one true God and to lead its own life without provoking the civil authorities of the Roman Empire. Even so, the Christian way of life offered a criticism of society which got through to pagan Romans, winning some to the Gospel but antagonizing others who condemned it as subversive. Only when actively persecuted did Christians challenge the state and incur the penalties of resistance to its totalitarian demands.

When Constantine emancipated Christianity and made it in effect the official religion of the Empire, the Church gained legal freedom to worship, to preach and lead its life openly. But it soon found itself hampered otherwise. The price of establishment was loss of independence to the state, and as its numbers grew rapidly its spirit was diluted. The Church's new predicament and its old habit of acquiescence blunted its social criticism.

Once the emperors and a large proportion of their subjects were Christians, the inconsistency between their conduct in church, where they worshipped as equals, and their conduct outside, where some were masters and others slaves, was felt; but it was not felt keenly enough to disturb consciences deeply. So ancient and universal was the practice of slavery, and so much was it the foundation of the economy of the world, that as an institution it was thought to be rather in accordance with than contrary to nature, men being what they are. Popes and bishops did not denounce slavery; but neither did they accept it without demur. They used the Church's position of influence to obtain improvements in the conditions of slaves, in particular legal recognition of their right to marry and form stable unions. They encouraged owners to treat their slaves with humanity and even to free them gratuitously as a great act of charity. The Church effected social change, but very slowly. Slavery lingered on until by the tenth century it was replaced by feudalism.

Feudalism the Church accepted as it had slavery, only more positively. For although the serf was not a free man, he was not a slave, merely another man's chattel. Though tied to his lord and subject to feudal service, the serf was accorded elementary human rights for himself and his wife and family. To that extent feudal society acknowledged the dignity of the human person, and the Church gave its support by underpinning feudal rights and duties with religious sanctions.

But as the popes became kings of central Italy and the bishops princes over their regions, the Church was made a pillar of the feudal establishment and a force against social and political change. In the late Middle Ages when commerce eroded the rigid structure of feudal society and roused aspirations for freedom, the higher clergy resisted the emancipation movement which the clerks and mendicant friars supported and led (Cf. J. Jusserand, *English Wayfaring Life in the Middle Ages*, London 1891, pp. 279-80, 287-90). They opposed it on the ground that emancipation would undermine social order and stability and injure the Church. But they also had a vested interest in preserving a social structure which gave them wealth, prestige and power.

The mendicant friars, the best examplars of the evangelical spirit at that time, saw clearly that the desire for freedom so far from being contrary to the Gospel is supported by it. Many centuries were to pass before this truth was widely grasped and officially proclaimed in the Catholic Church. Nothing obscured it more than the attachment of the papacy to temporal power and authoritarian government. Later events also darkened vision. The Reformation, which broke with the religious tradition of the past, and the Revolution, which threw off the social tradition as well, were strong inducements to intransigent conservatism in a Church which was the incarnation of the one and the chief agent of the other.

However, the religious and political trends which broke up Christendom and produced nation states and national churches posed anew the question of the basis and limits of civil authority and led to a development of thought which laid the foundations of contemporary Catholic social doctrine.

In the thirteenth century Aquinas held that rulers acquire civil authority from God as a trust to fulfil; that subjects owe obedience only in so far as rulers govern in the common good; and that constitutional monarchy offers the best hope of good government. In the sixteenth century Bellarmine and Suarez carried the argument on to further conclusions. They argued that rulers derive their authority from God indirectly, through consent of the people; that if rulers overstep the limit to civil authority set by the common good for which it is given, the people are entitled to withdraw consent and rebel; and that popular consent is the necessary basis under God of all civil authority. This last was a key idea which was to become the rationale of parliamentary democracy.

These ideas stemmed from the taproot of Christian social thought: the principle of the dignity and freedom of the human person, and its corollary, the common good as the purpose of civil authority. But in the struggle and confusion of the period of revolutionary change which produced the modern world, the ideas of Bellarmine and Suarez did not receive the attention which they merited. Instead, the Reformation and the Revolution produced in the Church in general and in the papacy in particular a defensive mentality closed to liberal views. Pope Pius IX in his *Syllabus of Errors* (1864) went so far as to condemn them as wrong in principle. But that was the verdict of a mind embittered by experience of the illiberalism of so many 'Liberals' and overwhelmed with anxiety about the Papal States. The only doctrinal significance of the condemnation was its implied denial that freedom is the supreme value. The point needed to be made. But if it was central to his protest Pius IX did not make his meaning clear.

In regard to this as to other points Pope Leo XIII reinstated the older and genuine tradition of Christian social doctrine, but as represented by Aquinas rather than as developed by Bellarmine and Suarez. Not until the world was again menaced by the totalitarian state in the twentieth century, as it had been in the sixteenth, did the ideas of Bellarmine and Suarez gain currency and development in official Catholic thought. Against Communism and Nazism and Fascism Pope Pius XI defended human dignity and freedom. In the darkest days of the second world war Pope Pius XII anticipated the Declaration of Human Rights which UNO was later to issue. But only in the time of Pope John XXIII and the Second Vatican Council did the Catholic Church definitely throw off its attitude of reserve towards the modern world and pass over from defence of human rights to promotion of human liberties.

In place of errors Pope John listed hopeful signs of the times: a deepening appreciation of human dignity and freedom; a rejection of all forms of discrimination based on class, nation, race, sex and creed; the aspiration of all peoples to political emancipation and self-government. This change of attitude and emphasis was confirmed by the Second Vatican Council and led to important doctrinal developments. One appears in the *Declaration on Human Freedom*. Religious freedom is stated to be a matter of fundamental right and not of mere expediency. Therefore religious toleration is now approved in principle as well as in practice and is claimed for every person whatsoever. Another appears in the Council's conception of the common good. This is defined no longer statically as the wellbeing of society but dynamically as the sum of conditions which enable men to progress together, developing their potentialities to the full. Such a conception obviously favours political liberalism.

In short, human dignity emerges from the documents of the Second Vatican Council as the cardinal value which the Church, as 'sign and safeguard of the human person' (*CCMW* 76), is committed to attest. It does so by promoting freedom for men to exercise personal responsibility in every sphere of life, including religion and politics.

For this remarkable swing by the Catholic Church from cold suspicion towards civil liberty and popular government in the nineteenth century to warm approval in the twentieth two major causes may be assigned. One has been its contrasting experience in the meantime of religious vigour under democracy and of religious suffocation under autocracy; the other has been the freedom which from the loss of its temporal power the Church has gained at its centre to pass disinterested judgment on political liberty as experienced in many different countries. The change has been one of development influenced by a varied experience, not one of basic principle. As it now stands Catholic social theory accords with the thought of Bellarmine and Suarez, which is in the main Christian tradition, and carries it on further.

* * * * *

The course of doctrinal change exemplified in these instances has evidently not been a mere substitution of one position for another as expediency has dictated. For the changes have resulted from a continual attempt to apply in changing social conditions a basic moral principle expressed in the Gospel in the precept of brotherly love and service.

From the first it was understood that in economic terms the precept requires men to share the goods of the earth in such a way that nobody lacks the means to support himself and his family decently, according to the standards of the day. Later it came to be seen that in political terms it means that the community must afford all its members opportunity to live as citizens. Step by step, in response to new conditions and needs, these notions of economic and political justice were enlarged to include also the means to personal development and freedom to play an active part in public affairs.

How in particular situations the sharing is to be done on a long-term policy for the common good, and what measure of freedom can be permitted if society is to survive as an organized community, are technical questions. With such the Church has not been directly concerned. Its concern has quite properly been with moral questions: whether the policy of civil authorities and the conduct of the public meet the requirements of the Gospel. In such matters, after mature theological investigation and due consultation, the final decision lies, in Catholic belief, with the pope and bishops, the appointed guardians of sound doctrine (Tit 1.9). They as a body are the official teachers of Christ's Church. Out of their judgements and theological discussion of the questions and answers Catholic social theory has grown.

Jesus Christ promised his followers the guidance of the Holy Spirit (Jn 14.25-6). How the Holy Spirit guides the Church is to be understood not so much by means of theological theory as of historical investigation. The evidence shows that the guidance of the Spirit has not exempted the Church from the ordinary process of learning laboriously by experience, study and debate. The history of Catholic social thought is a record of cautious advance in breadth and depth, with periods of hesitation, interruption, retrogression and resistance to change. Its course has been like a rough and winding passage through rapids rather than a steady glide along a straight and placid stream. The boat has gone forward, not because all of the crew have pulled together at the oars in confident unison, but because a few of them have seen further ahead and have somehow steered it safely through.

Errors of theory, failures in judgement of fact, and the tension referred to above (p. 107), have retarded but have not prevented permanently a genuine development of social doctrine. At times the development has been prodded by secular ideas and movements. From them, as is now frankly acknowledged (*CCMW* 44), the Church has greatly profited. However, the chief factor has been the effort, sometimes flagging but again and again renewed, to live by the principle of brotherly love and service. Through the centuries this has led to a growing appreciation of the fundamental dignity and equality of men and of their need of freedom for a full personal and social growth. Thus by trying to live by the Gospel in different conditions Christians have come by degrees to a fuller understanding of its social meaning. The Catholic Church has been encouraged and assisted by the efforts and achievements of other Churches (*ibid.*).

Christian social doctrine is moral doctrine. As such it offers neither a blue-print for social reconstruction nor a code of laws for society nor anything like a ready reckoner of answers to particular social problems, but a set of moral principles based on interpretation of the Gospel. These principles Christians have to understand and apply as best they can to the circumstances of their time.

* * * * *

Development can be expected to go on in the future, and in much the same way. Indeed, it is going on in the present, with concern for world justice and peace as the main growing point. This concern centres on the plight of millions of people in the underdeveloped countries, by convention collectively called 'the third world' (This is a misleading appellation, suggesting as a fact that the underdeveloped countries form a distinct world from the capitalist and communist worlds, and obscuring the fact that they form two thirds of the whole world). Voiced first by Pope John XXIII, then by the Second Vatican Council, its fullest expression appears in an encyclical letter on 'the development of peoples' (*Populorum Progressio*) addressed by Pope Paul VI in 1968 to 'all men of good will', focussing attention on a grave injustice of the present time.

In the present age of advanced technology people are everywhere restive. Conscious as never before of their human dignity and equality, they aspire to be free from grinding poverty, insecurity and oppression, to have the benefits of education and to share in responsibility: 'to have more, learn more, do more, and so to be more' (*PP* 6). These are legitimate aspirations. Yet the conditions of helpless destitution in which millions of the people are condemned to live their lives make them illusory for the nations of the third world. These nations, having gained political autonomy, find it impossible to achieve a corresponding economic growth and to play a dignified part in the community of nations.

This situation is justly described by Pope Paul as scandalous. The demand of justice and charity is clear. The strong nations, being highly developed and endowed, are under a moral obligation to use their resources and skill to help weak nations to grow strong enough to stand on their own feet and contribute as equals to the welfare and progress of mankind. It is therefore the duty of Christians and all men of conscience to alert public opinion and to apply pressure on governments to act in order to bring about a more equitable distribution of wealth and power among nations, and so secure world peace through world justice.

What is new in the encyclical is not so much its extension of the concept of justice to cover international economics and politics as its understanding of what justice between nations means in the world of today. It means that national policies and international agreements and trade must be governed by brotherhood and not by self-interest as the primary value. The primacy of self-interest serves only the purposes of neo-colonialism and economic imperialism. It will inevitably result in the continued economic exploitation and political domination of the weak nations by the strong. Contrariwise, a sense of the brotherhood of men would serve to bring about a fairer distribution of wealth and power and to create a new and just international order to the lasting benefit of all.

The message of *Populorum Progressio* is not utopian. It demands radical change in international affairs, but change of a kind which some nations have already made in their home affairs in order to achieve equity for all their citizens and compassion for the weak and deprived. With obvious truth the encyclical insists that international justice is the prerequisite of international peace. Its assertion that the primary value and motive in international affairs should be the brotherhood of men will commend itself not only to Christians and other religious men but also to all reasonable people who can rise above merely selfish considerations. If applied as a guiding principle in international affairs, the conception of the family or brotherhood of nations would go a long way towards correcting economic and political injustice and establishing lasting world peace.

Its effect on ourselves would be far-reaching. We could not, with a good conscience, be capitalists who exploit the resources of underdeveloped countries principally for the profit of investors abroad; or be shareholders who, provided that we receive our dividends, are quite unconcerned about the conduct of business and the wages and conditions of the indigenous workers whose labour contributes to our profits; or be consumers of food and goods at prices kept down by sweated labour in producing countries; or in any other way be sharers in the economic benefits of exploitation and imagine that in so doing we are not party to it. We could not in good faith make our own national economic growth and high standard of living the overriding consideration in our trading relations with the third world or with countries whose rulers hold some of the people in subjection for the advantage of others of privileged race, nation or class. If citizens of these countries, we could not accept their policies and practices as morally tolerable and omit to do what is possible to change them.

Significantly, the traditional Catholic doctrine concerning the morality of revolution noted in Chapter 4 reappears in the encyclical after a long period of eclipse. The reference to it, though brief, serves to dispel any illusions about the contemporary situation. It heavily underscores the injustice suffered by whole populations, the temptation for them to have recourse to violent revolution, and the menace it constitutes to world peace. Those who suffer injustice are warned that revolutionary uprisings notoriously tend to produce worse evils than those they seek to cure. But at the same time those responsible for their suffering are reminded that in standard Catholic doctrine there can be moral justification for revolution in cases of manifest and long-standing tyranny which gravely violates fundamental human rights and greatly harms the common good of the country (*PP* 30,31).

Nothing could testify more clearly to Pope Paul's sympathetic appreciation of the injustice suffered by millions of people today in the third world and elsewhere, and of the urgent need to correct it. He therefore pleads for an economic and technological revolution. More important still, he calls for 'a new humanism which will enable contemporary man to find himself again' (*PP* 20,42). Pope Paul adds, perhaps against the attempt of some to propagate a secularist and atheist human-ism, that to succeed the new humanism must take in not only man's relation to man but also his relation to God. He ends with an appeal to Catholics, all Christians, all who honour God, and all men of good will to 'open up the paths leading to mutual assistance among peoples, a deepening of human knowledge, an enlargement of heart, and a more brotherly way of living within a truly universal human society' (*PP* 85). The spirit if not the letter is that of the Gospel.

* * * * *

Already *Populorum Progressio* is being left behind as inadequate by critics of 'developmentalism'. Significantly, the criticism emanates from a part of the third world where the anguish of economic exploitation and political oppression is most acute and where the need to relate the Gospel directly to the sufferings of the deprived and downtrodden masses is felt to be most urgent.

In the experience of Latin America, and indeed of the third world generally, development has meant little more than policies of reform which leave the structures of society intact, and international programmes of aid and trade which continue the economic dependence of the poor nations on the rich nations of the world. The growth of the indigent is geared to the expansion of the affluent. Consequently, despair of development has led to its rejection and to conflict with the authorities in state and Church who resist the movement for change of a radical kind.

Among the Catholic clergy a growing number of young pastors of the suffering masses have come to the conclusion that what the third world needs, and what in the circum-stances the Gospel itself demands, is not development within the established order of society but liberation from it. Liberation and a just social order, they contend, will not come from above nor from outside. They must be won by the masses themselves by means of a revolutionary movement of thought and political action. In the current situation fidelity to the Gospel requires that Christians aid and abet this movement, that the Church provide the inspiration, and that the bishops permit not only laymen but also clerics the option of revolutionary involvement.

Accused by their opponents of being Marxist and not Christian at heart, these radical thinkers insist that their ideas and aims are evangelical. In support of this claim they are working out a 'theology of liberation' (Cf. G. Gutierrez, *A Theology of Liberation: History, Politics and Salvation.* London 1974). Its main contention, put very briefly, is that since the history of man and the history of salvation are fundamentally one history, and since sin is at root egotism and alienation from God and other men, every struggle against the exploitation of men by men is a partial and approximate liberation from sin and realization of communion with God and with other men. Every effort to create a just and liberating society is therefore a work of salvation, although not the whole of salvation.

Whether or not this theology of liberation will make a lasting contribution to Christian social thought and practice, it is premature to say. Fundamentally it is a critical presentation of the challenge and meaning of the Gospel in the Latin American situation. It is more accurately described as a theological argument for radical thought and action in a particular situation than as a theology claiming general validity. However, its influence is likely to be wide and strong, for good reason. Its spirit of compassion for the millions of deprived and oppressed people in the world today, and its theological argument for radical change in social structures, have the force of prophetical utterance. Our consciences are disturbed. We are induced to see that the attempts we have so far made to cure the world of its social evils are superficial: far short of what the Gospel demands of us. Though the city of God is not to be identified with the city of man, the change of heart required to enter the city of God, if genuine, will move us to make a corresponding change in our society and its structures today and not tomorrow.

INDEX